Millennial Style

ALIYYAH I. ABDUR-RAHMAN

Millennial Style

The POLITICS OF EXPERIMENT IN CONTEMPORARY AFRICAN DIASPORIC CULTURE

Duke University Press *Durham and London* 2024

Project Editor: Lisa Lawley
Designed by Courtney Leigh Richardson
Typeset in Warnock Pro, Canela Text, and Trade Gothic LT Std by Copperline Book Services

Library of Congress Cataloging-in-Publication Data
Names: Abdur-Rahman, Aliyyah I., author.
Title: Millennial style : the politics of experiment in contemporary African diasporic culture / Aliyyah I. Abdur-Rahman. Description: Durham : Duke University Press, 2024. | Includes bibliographical references and index.
Identifiers: LCCN 2023037610 (print)
LCCN 2023037611 (ebook)
ISBN 9781478030201 (paperback)
ISBN 9781478025955 (hardcover)
ISBN 9781478059196 (ebook)
Subjects: LCSH: African diaspora in literature. | African diaspora in art. | American literature—African American authors—History and criticism. | African American arts—21st century. | Politics and culture—United States—History—21st century. | Psychic trauma. | Womanism. | Queer theory.
Classification: LCC NX512.3.A35 A25 2024 (print) |
LCC NX512.3.A35 (ebook) | DDC 700.89/96—dc23/eng/20231103
LC record available at https://lccn.loc.gov/2023037610
LC ebook record available at https://lccn.loc.gov/2023037611

Cover art: Virginia Chihota, *Ndouya Kangani kuti undigamuchire? (How often will I come till you accept me?)*, 2019. Double-sided printed serigraph on archival cotton paper with silicone billboard, 50⅜ × 33⅞ in. Courtesy of the artist and Tiwani Contemporary Gallery.

TO KAMILAH,
for changing everything

TO ISA,
for always

CONTENTS

Millennial Style

INTRODUCTION

TOWARD A RADICAL THEORY OF THE BLACK AVANT-GARDE

What becomes possible when blackness wonders and wanders in the world, heeding the ethical mandate to challenge our thinking, to release the imagination, and to welcome the end of the world as we know it, that is, decolonization, which is the only proper name for justice?
—DENISE FERREIRA DA SILVA

It follows that black freedom is embedded within an economy of race and violence and unfolds as an indeterminate impossibility.
—KATHERINE MCKITTRICK

The endeavor is to recover the insurgent ground of these lives.
—SAIDIYA HARTMAN

RUINED

The poem begins with ash and ends in song in search of a language and a name. In the fourth section of the poetry book that doubles as the biography of an unnamed, black, queer southern boy, Saeed Jones's poem "Postapocalyptic Heartbeat" tells of life after ruin, insurgent life repeating itself after each and every predictable, awful demise. Jones's collection *Prelude to Bruise* reads like a gorgeous kaleidoscope of impressions—bits of narrative here and there—that invoke and inflect the sounds and colors and sensations of horror and loss. Many of the poems grapple with the difficult formation of an "I" seemingly damned or destined never to become one. The southern queer black subject of *Prelude* is simply called Boy. Bending and breaking, ceasing and beginning again, examining and meandering, unfolding and innovating, Boy does emerge somehow, unapologetic and resplendent. "Postapocalyptic Heartbeat" stands out from the other poems in the collection for its insinuation of the black communal and collective, for its allusion to the historical and always-present peril of black life. This poem evokes the devastations of isolation and invasion; snuffed-out life in militarized zones; ritualized lynching; bodies thrown overboard and out of windows; world-ruining empire. The poem takes the form of direct address and longs for a second person, who is at once an individual intimate and a collective audience, gone or yet to come:

> Drugged, I dreamed you a plume of ash
> great rush of wrecked air
> through the towns of my stupor.
>
> ....
>
> I saw us breathing on the other side of *after*.[1]

Opening at the site of wreckage, presumably in the aftermath of catastrophe, breath. Contaminated by ash that is simultaneously a life-giving other (the poem's "you"), bursting air pulsates through the deadened subject and its abandoned remembrances, "the towns of my stupor," to produce a vision of insurgent life, gathered, "us breathing on the other side of after."[2]

In content and arrangement, "Postapocalyptic Heartbeat" reaches for and records a directive, a map, a strategy, a guideline for existences bound and threaded by catastrophe. "I didn't exactly mean to survive myself," the speaker in the poem discloses after repeated self-willed falls from windows. After each fall, the speaker's audacious—if barely audible—heartbeat reflects the subtleties of black living in ruin without end.

> After ruin,
>
> after shards of glass like misplaced stars,
> after dredge
>
> after the black bite of frost: you are the after,
>
> ....
>
> a song in a dead language.[3]

The broken shards, which bespeak the shattering of something formerly integrated and whole, are nonetheless beauteous and luminescent like stars—

though these displaced and disordered stars are not those of the shared sky. Frostbitten flesh is flesh that has frozen to death. The secret of the speaker's perseverance is clearly not to be found in his singular battered self, nor in the numerous wrecked cities of his past, but in the arrival of "you," simultaneously his love(r) and his people. By collectivizing the speaker's journey, "Postapocalyptic Heartbeat" implies that, as death does not undo itself, but may be reconstituted and managed in song and memory, there is neither redemption nor reparation for black subjects after ruin. The Middle Passage, racial slavery spanning continents and lasting centuries, the intractability of racism as logic and force for disparately dealing out death and life, mass black impoverishment and immobilization, the slow and steady liquidation of black populations the world over—these cannot be firmly settled in the temporality of the past or the prior.[4] Ruin hijacks chronological time, nullifies normative temporalities, withholds the promise of closure or fulfillment, and negates redemptive futurities. For black subjects, after ruin, there is only relation, repetition, and the beautification of remains.[5]

I open with this brief critical encounter with Saeed Jones's "Postapocalyptic Heartbeat" to illuminate generally the concerns of this book and to indicate the speculative orientation of its scholarly and creative methods. As Jones narrativizes the burgeoning life of a black queer southern boy not in literary prose but via abstract poetics, *Millennial Style: The Politics of Experiment in Contemporary African Diasporic Culture* explores the deployment of aesthetic experiments in black cultural production to represent political annihilation, social ruin, and abbreviated black life in the decades since African Americans gained (yet again) formal equality before the law. Like Jones's poem, this book is a map—or, rather, its method is mapping. Its cartography stretches, sketches, and interweaves elements of the genealogical, the material, the political, the epistemological, and the cultural to say something about living and aching—and the unyielding combination thereof—that come from being and being borne of the black.

The genesis of this study is a flash point, a brief moment of arrival and the promise of steady, settled life quickly beset by the usual crises, losses, and terrors that typify racialized existence and racist intransigence. It was in August some years ago now when eighteen-year-old Michael Brown was killed by the police in Ferguson, Missouri, his body left in the street for hours, his mother, somehow not deranged by grief, asking pedestrians and shocked onlookers not to circulate on social media the images of her dead child. Less than a year prior, queer activist women of color had taken to Twitter to decry the acquittal of Trayvon Martin's murderer, George Zimmerman, with the simple hashtag #BlackLivesMatter. It was the most compelling and most heart-wrenching speech act of the decade: the actuation of a wish, phenomenon, or ritual by virtue of its mere utterance. Black people across genders were dying at the hands of police, sometimes on camera—black death gone viral. African Americans mourned publicly; a nation erupted; a global conversation started.[6] Students on college campuses took over administration buildings to demand recognition of the Global Movement for Black Lives. Everywhere people were in the streets, in protest, and on social media, with distressed urgency. This time was unique in all of modern history by virtue of the black man in the office of the presidency of the United States. And yet it was the simple fact that Barack Obama and Michael Brown overlapped in nation and in time that I felt driven to accept, for once and for all, that things in this despicable, despicable place would never, ever really be better. The achievement of true equality, of the conditions, chances, and simple duration of black lives, would neither be secured nor guaranteed by any legislative achievement, juridical reform, or legal redress. The symbolic manifestation of racial equality, as embodied by an African American in the highest political office of the United States, did little to eradicate racism or to improve the psychosocial, material, and political conditions under which black lives are lived. Freedom would not come—at least not of the liberal democratic but stunningly close to white supremacist, neofascist kind—for those whose generational enslavement gave rise to the shape of Euro-American democracy; the purported ascent of reason over godliness; the racialist, racist contours of the human; the emergence of the citizen (as the proper subject and beneficiary of liberal governance) as white, propertied, patriarchal.

Never in modernity—this period that founded new empires and global economies through the transatlantic shipment, sale, and forced labor of millions and millions of Africans—have we secured or even approached durable black freedom. No language has been suitable to describe it; no political party or movement has succeeded in sustainably achieving it. We live now in the chronological future, in the afterward and the aftermath, of black liberation struggles undertaken over two centuries.[7] Nevertheless, so many of us are murdered—shot in homes shielding babies, strangled to death in chokeholds, tasered and pulverized into corpses—by US state agents. Some of these deaths are caught on camera, globally disseminated, and viewed ad nauseum. But neither massive witnessing nor global protest has prevented or curtailed the sickening accumulation of black corpses. There are so many of us, captured and encaged by the millions, who are immobilized, unseen, dying slowly. Those of us who are not warehoused often live and raise children, themselves always susceptible to capture or removal or early demise, in food deserts that are simultaneously environmental wastelands. So many of us have been barred from suitable housing, equitable health care, utilizable education, decent employment, and an inviolable self-concept. And so few of us have ever experienced life as a safe and sustainable undertaking, enterprise, or even possibility.

Millennial Style is the culmination of a meditation that began that horrific season (which is perhaps all seasons) of dead black children and the resultant call, proclamation, plea for black lives to matter. It was around that time that my only child received the diagnosis of a devastating illness, chronic but not fatal. With intermittent trips to the hospital, a team of medical professionals on speed-dial, the energy to encounter repeated flare-ups like the first occurrence, the illness could be managed. His life would be impacted but not wholly dismantled, not lost altogether. But that wasn't really true, was it—an illness on top of racial blackness; burgeoning, brash masculinity; young adulthood; Muslim identity? Wouldn't a chronic illness, the condition of debilitated and attenuated living, further compound the vulnerability of one who belongs already to those targeted for early death within necropolitical, white supremacist regimes? Certainly, my child was (and is) in my locked grasp, but carceral logics, normative hypersurveillance, and militarized policing evolved decades ago at the intersection of the war on drugs and the war on terror could get a grip on both of us. I turned to the cultural producers, the writers, the visual artists, the beauty-makers, the transformers of and within the African diaspora and—with all of the language available to me and every bit of critical capacity brought to bear—I pleaded, "What's next? What now?" And they answered.

The late Nobel laureate Toni Morrison writes, "Certain kinds of trauma visited on people are so deep, so cruel, that unlike money, unlike vengeance, even unlike justice, or rights, or the good will of others, only writers can translate such trauma and turn sorrow into meaning, sharpening the moral imagination."[8] *Millennial Style* enlists contemporary black cultural production for the translation of trauma into meaning, for modalities of expression beyond the futility of political and politicized representation, for guidelines and guideposts to living in the ongoing catastrophe that characterizes black life in modernity. With combined interests in formal experiment and in movement—the movement of global capital, the transnational circulation and consumption of black images and black cultural products, the migratory patterns of African-descended people, and the philosophical linkage between unmooring and the attainment of (an always tenuous) individual agency—this book explores the ways in which desire and disaster, which seem in racial, relational, personal, and political terms to be coextensive phenomena, simultaneously shape and resist narrative and visual representation. The study pursued in this book is animated by two overarching questions: (1) What compels the impulse toward the experimental, the avant-garde, and the abstract among contemporary African diasporic cultural producers who are generally expected to represent the truth of racial harm and to (imaginatively) remediate it?; and (2) How might abstractionist expressive modes—that is, in contrast to realist or mimetic modes of representation—conjure and convey the tactics and nuances of black sociality, solidarity, and survival in modern contexts best characterized as disasters without end?

Millennial Style proceeds via an interrogation of the interrelation of political terror, social abjection and aesthetic abstraction in contemporary African diasporic cultural production. This book is thus an earnest—if at times heart-heavy—attempt at reckoning with black art- and world-making practices that take seriously the denial of progressive change or futural improvement for black subjects living in and after ruin (of our times, of our lives). It tracks the decline of mimetic realism as the presumed most suitable and most reliable modality of representing racial injury and of imagining (and iterating the promises of) political remedy. Following the expressive forms it analyzes, *Millennial Style* looks beyond aggrieved appeals to the state (rendered corrupt, defunct, inaccessible, or inoperable) for social remedy, sustainable material conditions, and political redress under conditions of normalized state-manufactured ruin. It proceeds with suspicion about sentimentalism as the predominant affect underpinning (and generated by) black cultural expression, particularly in literature and visual art manifestly oriented toward socioracial, material, and political improvement for black subjects. Throughout the analyses that fill this book, I challenge literalist reading practices that treat black cultural production sociologically—that is, reading for supposed truths of racial subjectivity and collectivized racist injury and inattentive to the formal innovations and stylistic praxes of African diasporic literature and visual art. I refute, moreover, cultural criticism that is presumptive (or consumptive, really) about the availability of black subjective interiors and the transparency of black life-worlds.

Taking its cue from and building upon Phillip Brian Harper's provocative contention that "abstractionism [is] the most powerful modality for Black representation," *Millennial Style* advances Harper's account of black abstraction by conceptualizing its practice in specific relation to racial abjection and by tracking specific aesthetic modalities or maneuvers within and beyond US borders.[9] I theorize four specific aesthetic strategies or expressive praxes—Black Grotesquerie, Hollowed Blackness, Black Cacophony, and the Black Ecstatic—that, while neither exclusive nor exhaustive, have become, I argue, the most predominant and pervasive aesthetic modes across literature, visual art, and film in contemporary black cultural production of high experiment. I focus specifically on these aesthetic modes for inquiry and theory due to their unique capacity to signify and operate multiply, as innovative expressive techniques, affective resonances, relational models, and as radical, if subtle, political interventions. Via recombinant art techniques such as substitution, collage, contortion, and inversion, *Black Grotesquerie* renders the boundary between black living and black dying porous and mutable; it shifts the concern of black life from politics and performances of survival to gestures and technologies of continuance (of keeping on) by textualizing catastrophe as the context for black being and by materializing the preservation of blackness within and beyond ruin. *Hollowed Blackness* conveys the ubiquitous experiences of pursuit, capture, and containment for black subjects, alongside the emotional strain of hollowness or hollowing out. In black expressive texts, the configuration of *Black Hollows* advances a black abolitionist aesthetic that alters liberationist ideologies of fugitivity by reimagining its primary architecture from the outward and external outdoors to the interior and internal hollow. *Black Cacophony* is the enraged, despairing, lust-filled, deranged, nonmelodic sounding off of black pain and black want in African diasporic literature. It is a tactic of textual representation that exposes both the insufficiency and superfluity of language for capturing exploited or discarded black life while insisting, in its sentient soundings, that such life matters. Across literary and cinematic platforms, *the Black Ecstatic* reveals willful exuberance to be the affective disposition and relational ethic that enables black life and liberation in the midst of ongoing terror, crisis, and loss. It is a queer expressive modality that aestheticizes black mystery and synthesizes fleeting moments of black communion into an exhilarating eternality.

What remains of this introduction unfolds in pursuit of three goals: first, to offer, in conversation with black feminist and black queer studies scholars, a theory of black avant-gardist practice that commits radically to an improved world for the planet's most devastated, injured, and neglected populations; second, to highlight the affective and relational undercurrents of black lifeworlds as they are imaginatively rendered by the assembly of cultural producers in *Millennial Style*; and, third, to describe in specific detail the four pervasive, abstractionist aesthetic strategies in post–civil rights black expressive culture (grotesquerie, hollowness, cacophony, ecstasy) that relate and respond to new (updated and abstracted) regimes of globalized racial terror. These four aesthetic strategies, or expressive modes, offer a glimpse into the tactics of black solidarity, sociality, and survival that subtend contemporary African diasporic art forms and constitute the core inquiry of *Millennial Style*.

BLACK EXPERIMENT

Analyzing work by a rich array of contemporary black authors and visual artists—including Toni Morrison, Wangechi Mutu, Saeed Jones, Colson Whitehead, Alexandria Smith, Alexis de Veaux, Essex Hemphill, and Barry Jenkins, among others—*Millennial Style* studies the ways in which contemporary black cultural producers interrogate realism as the proper artistic modality for conjuring black life in the post–civil rights moment. These cultural practitioners resist, I argue, the requirement for racially affirmative portrayals of black people and manifestly politicized accounts of black suffering. In other words, their aesthetic experiments critique the politics of representation, even as they register the life-diminishing impacts of racialized state violence in the current moment. I show how these visual artists and writers do this by rupturing, renovating, and resignifying the formal features of traditional protest literature and visual propaganda—or, to put it plainly, by deploying and further developing the black avant-garde. The avant-garde engenders strange and at times sublime aesthetic encounters that summon uncommon affective responses, different cognitive capacities, and alternative hermeneutics. The black avant-garde iterates an aesthetic repudiation of spectacularity—in its record of ruin *and* promise of progress—in twenty-first-century black expressive culture.

That the principle evaluative metric applied to black cultural forms is political instrumentality, and that social protest has historically conditioned African American cultural production, are virtually axiomatic critical assessments to this point. The long-standing mandate for racial authenticity as a principal evaluative criterion in black expressive culture has dual components: racially affirmative (or racially "real") representation, and a set of generic conventions, dating back to the slave narrative, that infuses political aspiration with expressive form. In many ways, the slave narrative inaugurated African Americans' formal entrance into American letters. As a body of literature that responded to the most extreme form of corporeal, civic, and social death, the slave narrative was manifestly politically motivated. Its content and its form—specifically, the authenticating documents that precede the narrative proper, attestations of authorial competence and sincerity, and frequent deviations from the central narrative to detail atrocities regularly practiced on slave plantations—attest to the humanity, the civility, and the moral and intellectual capacity of black people. In documenting in linear fashion one enslaved subject's journey from bondage to freedom, the slave narrative purported, and in every way attempted, to represent the lives and political aspirations of the entire race, to get and to remain free. Despite the abolition of slavery, the persistence of lethal forms of race-based socioeconomic and political exclusion, with their concomitant effect of African Americans' psychological and literal annihilation, have kept the commitment to black social advancement and positive racial representation foremost in black expressive culture.

While, in the twenty-first century, the logics and implications of race have supposedly shifted, continued antiblack state violences and the systematic discard of impoverished black people expose racism as a lethal apparatus of psychosocial and material asymmetry that supersedes the legal remedy of recognition politics. Notably, the signal achievement of the civil rights movement was the inclusion of African Americans in formal US politics, made manifest through voting rights and the greater representation of black people in all spheres of legislative governance. Increased black participation in the formal mechanisms of liberal democratic politics over the last half-century has not guaranteed the removal of institutional, civic, socioeconomic, and psychic barriers to black American advancement. The mere presence of black congressional members, mayors, governors, and the like neither demonstrates nor ensures meaningful sociopolitical transformation in which the most vulnerable racialized subjects gain conditions of ordinary thriving. This book recognizes that representations of political crises in black life no longer inhere in *or adhere to* established literary or (visual) media forms. Rather, as forms of racialized economic, social, and political harm have itself become less formal and more abstract—the move, for example, from legal segregation to segregation produced via educational disparities, deindustrialization, redlining practices—the aesthetic techniques and expressive modalities used to tell stories of black lives and aspirational freedoms have themselves become more abstract.[10] It is, therefore, no longer critically useful or viable to invest verisimilitude in black cultural production with the potency and the promise of inclusive political representation.

In "Mathematics, Black Life," Katherine McKittrick compellingly describes how blackness structures the economics and the sociopolitical systems of existence, semiexistence, and nonexistence in racialized modernity. The mathematics in her title refers to the quantification of black life, the brutal economics—"breathless numbers . . . the mathematics of the unliving"—that undergird racial enslavement, mass warehoused black life unto/until death, scientific and statistical data recording lessened and lost black life, and the sketchy archival remains of black persons and populations.[11] Characterizing blackness in modernity, she writes:

> While the tenets and lingering histories of slavery and colonialism produced modernity as and through Blackness, this sense of time-space in interrupted by a more weighty and seemingly more truthful . . . underside—where Black is naturally malignant and therefore worthy of violation; where Black is violated because Black is naturally violent; where Black is naturally less-than-human and starving to death and violated; where Black is naturally dysselected, unsurviving, swallowed up; where Black is same and always and dead and dying; where Black is complex and difficult and too much to bear and violated.[12]

McKittrick captures a historically imposed racial hierarchy so deep and abiding that it has the power to delineate simultaneously subjecthood and its abrogation. Modernity's principal promises are a progressive temporal schema, perpetually advancing and accretive, and the subject's right to accumulation and increase in and over progressive time. The modern conception of the subject is ultimately possessive and propertied where being and having and taking collide. Rooted in transatlantic slavery, the conquest and reterritorializing of the globe, and the management or removal of its various populations, the subject and the white emerge in modernity at the same time and as the same thing. On the other hand, the black, the imminently killable nonsubject, is stuck in stasis, occupying the status of metaphysical negation, always vulnerable to demise or disappearance or to being taken or had. McKittrick invokes the inherent vulnerability of blackness as "violated"—in life and, in her language, on repeat.

Millennial Style pursues two objectives: the development of an analytics of blackness that does not replicate its violent negation, and the performance of expressive modalities of blackness that do not reiterate the murderous frames of its capture. I consider the importance of understanding the economization of black life—statistical enumeration, recorded documents, lists and ledgers, archival residue of black demise—for these provide the bases for political complaint, creative strategies of survival, the reformation of relational ethics, and insurrectionist ideals of black study. Ultimately, however, emancipatory schemas do not inhere in accounts of the black dead and dying, whether historical or statistical. "It follows," McKittrick surmises, "that black freedom is embedded within an economy of race and violence and unfolds as an indeterminate impossibility."[13] For black liberative possibility to manifest, its grammars and tactics must be nondeterministic, unanticipated, experimental—implausible, even. More specifically, within the realm of expressive culture, to dismantle the given order, to undo the effects of ongoing catastrophe, to expose the particularity of each successive disaster, and to etch pathways to implausibly free black futures require the summons and practice of the black avant-garde.

I am cognizant of the risk of using *avant-garde* as a term for conveying innovative artistic endeavors and de/reforming maneuvers within contemporary African diasporic aesthetic practice. Within the discipline of art history and criticism in particular, the term typically designates Euro-American art that, while profoundly rejecting the status quo, also eschews meaningful interaction with the everyday, the popular, the social.[14] Implied in the designation *avant-garde* is nonreferential aesthetic experimentation that is manifestly disinterested in or disengaged from societal concerns and political grammars. The term is also often associated with white cultural elitism—some of which exploited the so-called primitivism of black cultural forms—of the modernist era. My conceptual recoding of *the avant-garde* updates and politicizes the term via the modifier *black* to reflect the strategic deployment of abstract, antirepresentational practices within contemporary African diasporic cultural expression.

I regard the elasticity and broad applicability of the avant-garde in part by thinking with Hal Foster, who disassociates the avant-garde from any particular movement, time period, artistic strategy, or expressive style. He defines the avant-garde broadly as experimental cultural production that encodes a radical rearticulation of the artistic vis-à-vis the political. Foster contends:

> The avant-garde is defined in two ways only—as vanguard in a position of radical innovation, or as resistant, in a position of stern refusal to the status quo. Typically, too, the avant-garde is understood to be driven by two motives alone: the transgression of a given symbolic order (as with surrealism) or the legislation of a new one (as with Russian Constructivism). However, the avant-garde that interests me here is neither *avant* nor rear in those senses; rather, it is imminent in a caustic way. Far from heroic, it does not pretend that it can break absolutely with the old order or found a new one; instead, it seeks to trace fractures that already exist within the given order, to pressure them further, to activate them somehow. Far from defunct, this avant-garde is alive and well today.[15]

Rather than regarding the avant-garde as a dated artistic movement, Foster emphasizes its imminence. He tempers its association with pure aesthetic innovation and complete societal disavowal. I am persuaded by Foster's contention that the avant-garde neither resolutely rejects the awful status quo with which it contends nor does it aim to wholly reinvent the world. Instead, the avant-garde pressures the present, exposing and exploring its (socioeconomic, psychic, cultural, political) fissures, disforming when not reforming them. I invoke the black avant-garde to name African diasporic cultural production of recent decades that scavenges sociopolitical wreckage, studies the preludes and afterwards of each successive disaster in black historico-political life, and innovates artistic practices that engage the ruined world and reveal how (always vulnerable, imminently killable) black subjects might continue to endure it.

While the majority of the literary, visual, and filmic texts that I explore were produced in the twenty-first century, its inquiry examines more broadly black cultural production following the civil rights movement. It is worth noting here that *Millennial* in the title of this book is not meant to signal expressive styles or strategies that belong exclusively to African diaspora production of the twenty-first century, though the overwhelming majority of the literature and visual art that I study are post-2000 productions; nor is the term meant to refer to aesthetic praxes developed and deployed exclusively by the millennial generation of black cultural producers—though some of the literary, visual, and filmic texts herein analyzed were indeed produced by black millennials. Rather, I use it to indicate the set of historical and political circumstances out of which both this generation *and* these aesthetic praxes emerge, most specifically the historical and political circumstances inaugurated by the Reagan era. Deploying *Millennial* as a historiographic rather than a generational or subjective classification allows me to avoid positing a vanguard that is presumably best poised to meet this moment's challenges. As a historical marker, *Millennial* delineates the notable socioeconomic and political shifts of the last century—specifically neoliberal retrenchment and neofascist ascendancy—that have shaped the current moment of societal and racist destruction.

The last two decades of the twentieth century witnessed the rise of multicultural discourse and multicultural representation in media and education alongside the steady withdrawal of civil rights gains, the erasure of social safety nets for marginalized and impoverished black and brown communities, financial deregulation, and the deleterious and robust rise of the prison industrial complex. The popularization of the discourse of multiculturalism and the emergence of the so-called culture wars in the 1980s obscured the aims of racial justice rooted in material redistribution and sociopolitical equity.[16] As inclusive politics increasingly implied tokenism and representative visibility, there was a concomitant abatement of any national commitment to the amelioration of the socioeconomic and psychic aftereffects of racial slavery and legal segregation, to equitable opportunity in all domains of human aspiration, and to reparative political inclusion. Resurgent white supremacy informed the policies of Reagan's administration, which dismantled social safety nets, defunded food and housing programs for impoverished people, and reversed critical civil-rights-era affirmative action legislation.[17] I encounter the (turn to the) twenty-first century as a period reflective of tremendous information, communication, and data technologies; the normalization of austerity measures and intensified material precarity for the masses; perpetual imperialist war on Muslims under the guise of the war on terror; domestic warfare against black and brown people instrumentalizing abusive policing and carceral containment; and the historic election of the first self-identified black president succeeded by a wholly unqualified and belligerent white supremacist one. And I proceed with the recognition that the groundwork for the conditions of the current century were laid by the political and economic policies, in the United States and abroad, of the decades that closed the last one.

My focus on the avant-garde refers to artistic production that gives rise to new aesthetic experiences, encourages thought restructuring, imagines alternative modes of sociality, and inspires unanticipated political interventions. A brief note on related terminology is useful here, though each of these terms will receive more in-depth treatment in subsequent chapters. I use the terms *experiment* and *experimentation* to delineate the general orientation, method, and approach to art. Rather than any attempt at verisimilitude or representing "the real," the writers and visual artists at the center of this study are practitioners of literary, visual, and filmic experiment. I use the terms *abstract, abstraction,* and *aesthetic abstraction* to comment on the literary and visual art objects themselves, to name the cumulative effect or style of the art produced. It is important to note that in this study abstract/abstractionism does not necessarily signify complete conceptualism. In the creative objects under consideration, there is generally some retention of the figural—by which I mean the evident subjective, bodily, material, historical, political referent or remnant—in the artwork produced. This referential retention is key to the aesthetic strategies of decomposition, estrangement, (re)assembly, disorder, resignification that drive artistic innovation and radical political imaginings in contemporary black expressive culture. I investigate the practices and poetics of structural ambiguity in imaginative texts of the black everyday that transgress and transform the boundaries among cultural production, social organization, and embodied and political life. Furthermore, I offer a conception of contemporary black life that reckons truly with the intricacies and continuities of political terror, a robust reappraisal of black aesthetic praxis, and a promiscuous reading of the archive of African diasporic cultural production in the twenty-first century.

UNDERCURRENTS

In an autobiographical essay written for *Ebony* magazine titled "Infinite Ache: My First Mother's Day without Her," Saeed Jones describes the first year of mourning he spent in the wake of his beloved mother's passing. She had died unexpectedly shortly before Mother's Day. Over the twelve months spread between the day assigned for honoring mothers, Jones struggled with perpetual, unbearable grief. "I would stand up and cry," he remembers, "until there was nothing to do but lay down and cry. I would wake up with tear streaks on my face and the moment I remembered why, I'd start crying again." Mourning her loss, finding new ways to manage her constant and forever goneness, was, for Jones, impossible. During that first year, he discovered that the magnitude of his suffering was matched only by the depth of the life-giving bond between his mother and her queer black boy; it also defined their new relation. I use the example of Saeed Jones's literary record of filial love to illustrate both the conceptualization and the deployment of black queerness as analytic and method in this book. What warrants emphasis here is how the powerful attachment undergirding this filial relation departs from the normative structures and affective ties of the heteropatriarchal household, offering an occasion for a thick and dexterous conception of queer/ness within African American relational rubrics and aesthetic praxes.

Jones's relationship with his mother yielded the most important blueprint for his being and for his queer black becoming. He characterizes the connection reconfigured by maternal death in terms of awe: "Awe at the undeniable fact that I will forever be the son of a fiercely beautiful woman. Awe at knowing just how exquisitely she prepared me to live and write my way into this world." Jones owns and celebrates the fact of this, using the occasion of Mother's Day to record textually the fierceness and the fearlessness of his mother. "Love, mother love in particular, is not free," he muses. He includes part of a letter his mother had written to him while he was a boy away at camp in which she'd said, "'I love you more than the air I breathe.'" When love is more powerful than breath, it entails great risk; it creates even as it attenuates life. Jones concludes, "A love like that is worth an infinite ache."[18] The love that sustains tenuous black living and yet calls for and culminates in interminable aching stretches in Jones's work black queerness beyond identity and individuated patterns of erotic desire. Following Jones, black queerness is deployed methodologically and hermeneutically in my readings of specific experimental black texts beyond the designation of specific erotic practices, subjectivities, or political agendas. Rather, black queerness enmeshes all manner of racialized being and longing with fluid temporalities, ethical affect, and suturing sociality.

Throughout *Millennial Style*, I proceed with the notion of the black as a sentient entity, a form of life, and a modality of living whose defining characteristic is that of nonpossession. By virtue of its undoing through the totalizing (embodied, social, and political) dispossession of enslavement and the violent temporal and geographic dislocations of the Middle Passage, the black emerges in modernity as a being divested of the right of and capacity for possession, including of normative attributes like sexuality and gender. In this book, as within black life-worlds generally, queerness signifies, on one hand, subjective and sexual formations and, on the other, affective and relational orientations. Black queerness is embodied—that is, operant and expressed through bodily forms, desires and movements—but uncontained by the fixtures of identitarian logics and the spatiotemporal limits of geographic boundedness and chronology. It is this broad understanding of black queerness that interests me and that informs my engagement with it as an episteme throughout *Millennial Style*. As Jafari Allen so powerfully reminds us, "Unbelonging is, paradoxically, powerfully constitutive."[19] At its most conceptually capacious and politically relevant (for me and for this study), black queerness designates forms and formulations of nonsovereign being, temporality unbound by teleology, and reparative sociality. Additionally, it makes each of these the basis for a new black critical discourse.

In *None Like Us: Blackness, Belonging, Aesthetic Life*, Stephen Best reassesses the scholarly inclinations and political orientations of black cultural criticism and interrogates the instrumentalization of historic racial injury as the foundation for black aesthetics, cultural belonging, and political endeavor in the present. Notably, his impassioned renunciation of "the melancholy affective history project that has prevailed in [African-American] cultural criticism" attends simultaneously to black cultural output and the academic disciplines that have been built around it.[20] Inspired by the work of Wendy Brown, Best cautions against forging US democratic projects that are reliant upon melancholic investments in histories of transatlantic slavery and the mobilization of "wounded attachments" to redress abominable racial harm.[21] He calls into question the intellectual and political utility of recuperative identitarian projects in African American cultural studies aimed at historical recovery, mythic black belonging, and (barely accomplished) racial advancement. Best urges ultimately for the disarticulation of black studies

> from the historical accretions of slavery, race, and racism, or from a particular commitment to the idea that the slave past provides a ready prism for understanding and apprehending the black political present. In spite of the many truths that follow our acceptance of slavery as generative of blackness, as productive of the background conditions necessary to speak from the standpoint of blackness, *None Like Us* begins in the recognition that there is something impossible about blackness, that to be black is also to participate, of necessity, in a collective undoing, if not, on the occasion that that should either fail or seem unpalatable, a self-undoing.[22]

Racial slavery and persistent, pervasive antiblackness shape the histories and impact the current life experiences and outcomes of black subjects. Best urges, nonetheless, more inventive reckonings with the fractures, losses, and impossibilities that, as a result, beset black subjects and black social life beyond any meaningful claim or capacity for restoration.

To get at the profound internal fragmentation and social unbelonging of blackness—its historic lack of a sustained and unified polity and the lack of integrated wholeness within black subjectivities—Best turns to queer theory, particularly its negative, anti-relational strain. In so doing, he assigns himself "the task of drawing out the connections between a sense of impossible black sociality... and strains of negativity that often have operated under the sign *queer*."[23] While I do not share Best's enthusiasm for anti-relational theories of subjective and social negation within queer studies as a framework for theorizing black desire (whether personal or political) that is alienated, unfounded, thwarted, impossible, I am, indeed, moved by his bold assessment that queerness underwrites any persuasive account of black radicality in contemporary African American cultural criticism. In this regard, Best's work joins, to my thinking, with recent work by such scholars as Kara Keeling, Tavia Nyong'o, and Mecca Jamilah Sullivan, that underscores the queer undercurrents of blackness.

In *Queer Time, Black Futures*, Kara Keeling examines the cultural deployment of the technology, imagination, and speculative futurities to picture black and queer liberation in the aftermath of racial slavery and in the midst of racial capitalism. Her reinstallation of the promise of freedom to come for vulnerable black and queer subjects—in time, after the future—proceed from theories of queer spatiotemporality. Keeling specifies the conceptual usage of queer in her study not in terms of ontology but of epistemology, concerned with "life and death questions of apprehension and value production."[24] Keeling's expansive and refigured notion of the queer foregrounds taxonomies of human valuation in the production of knowledge, providing an analytic linchpin for her investigation of race, temporality, and the financialization of human life. She writes:

> The production of "queer" is violent, material, and excessive to the management and control of sociability. "Queer" is palpable, felt as affect. It is also not only an imposition but simultaneously a becoming. . . . "Queer" is a long-haul proposition available in any-instant-whatever. Queer's proliferation of connections among disparate, qualitatively different things pile up, indifferent to its ability to measure or completely capture them. Capable of being modulated to the demands of Capital, queer nonetheless stubbornly works on and through bodies, establishing relations between them and thereby connecting them across time and space.[25]

Queerness is embodied in form and movement, gesture and shape. Although queerness is under the sway of capital, it can move in opposition to it. Furthermore, even as it escapes the normative dictates and confines of sociability, queerness can operate as potent connective tissue across social domains.

In her breathtaking book *The Poetics of Difference: Queer Feminist Forms in the African Diaspora*, Mecca Jamilah Sullivan studies the queer feminist poetics of black women writers across the African diaspora. Attentive to the ways in which black women authors throughout the diaspora writers have deployed the "nuantial" and "interstitial" to subvert the formal conventions and genres of literary expression, she theorizes distinct black queer feminist poetics—for example, the biomythic and choreopoetic—to show how they advance "complex, antinormative models of black womanhood that critique multiple power structures and interpretive conventions at once."[26] Sullivan intentionally weaves and unweaves the intersecting threads of black experience across numerous axes and arenas of difference, including sexuality, gender, history, geography. In so doing, she posits the importance of holding together black and queer historiography as a critical practice that attends to the always interimbricated, multifaceted, and reciprocal histories of black and queer life. She writes: "For many queer writers of the African diaspora, blackness and queerness are not separate identificatory markers; rather, they are contiguous signifiers of a difference that defines temporal and social experience. In their worlds, there cannot be black history without several forms of queerness, and there cannot be black queer survival without several concurrent black histories."[27]

Expansive, critically and politically generative concepts of queer/ness are rooted in genealogies of black thought. In *Afro-Fabulations: The Queer Drama of Black Life*, Tavia Nyong'o analyzes the methodologies and maneuvers of queer of color critical thought to articulate the gestures, patterns, praxes, and rhythms of black life in a viciously antiblack world. Nyong'o's study moves astutely past decades-long dichotomous debates within queer theory—specifically around anti-relationality and anti-normativity—by exposing the curated (and even whitewashed) genealogies of the field. Through both his critique and his citational practice, Nyong'o emphasizes "the place of theorists of color, and black theorists specifically, in the intellectual and political genealogy of what we now call queer theory."[28] He summons "the speculative powers of blackness, which are non-identitarian" to simultaneously broaden and sharpen critical and commonsense notions of the queer and to harness the aesthetic and political utility of queerness as long-standing features of black expressive culture and black liberative endeavor.[29]

Millennial Style examines experimental black aesthetics as a mode of queer art production, as the holding (or hoarding) of black mortal and material resources against the injuries and inevitabilities of social death, as the fashioning of relational ethics in the face of sociopolitical domination, as exuberant black diasporic world-building in perpetually perilous times. This study navigates the tension among theoretical strands of negativity and antisociality within queer studies; nihilistic structural critiques within black studies; and the material and political need for the vulnerable to find community and build solidarities. I turn to black avant-garde aesthetics as a rich reservoir for imagined enactments of an improved world for persons and populations that are subject to continual diminishment, discard, dissolution. These are the themes of numerous poems in Saeed Jones's *Prelude to Bruise*, particularly in the poems that conjure his mother. By depicting his mother as the blueprint for his formation, Jones records the constant vigilance—the impossible maneuvering on behalf of bequeathed but abjured black life—that defines black filial relations and that render them, in this time and place, both nonheteronormative and nonpatriarchal. In this stunning book of poetry, a chronicle of the burgeoning subjectivity of a southern black queer boy, it is the lost black mother that lends Jones's poetry its haunting edges and caressing reprieves. I conclude this section by lingering in those healing spaces. The title of this poem, "Mercy," is also the text of its intermittent one-lined stanzas:

> Her ghost slips into the room wearing nothing but the memory
> of a song; thin as a note lost in a little girl's throat,
>
> *mercy.*
>
> If fog had a sound
>
> if the moon decided to hold its breath
>
> if she ever heard the way I cry out in my sleep
>
> *mercy.*
>
> She knows I'm not well, sees the dark circling my eyes,
> one more inheritance,
>
> *mercy.*
>
> Her stare traces me
> and a hand reaches out but Mama, I don't know the words.[30]

In this poem the mother who has left the world, or who has been taken from it, finds a way to reverse the passage, to inhabit the rooms where her left-behind child is stuck in isolated, ceaseless grief. Even the legible inscription of falling apart—darkness encircling the eyes—is a treasured legacy. Transcending the passage of time and the finitude of death, the ghostly mother returns to restore and (re)shape her queer black son. She inspects and caresses her grown child. And, in so doing, the gone mother teaches him to resonate with mercy, to heal with mercy, to release with mercy. She guides him to the apprehension and appreciation that things are impermanent; they come and they go. And in that rush of movement, the push and pull of what passes by and passes on, what we can do, and perhaps must do, is to anchor ourselves and one another with(in) mercy.

AGAINST REPRESENTATION

Millennial Style turns to literature, visual art, and cinema produced by vulnerable, imminently killable black subjects, and the marginalized among even them—black people from across the diaspora who have suffered racist injury, displacement, gendered harm, confinement, disease, debility, shortened and stolen life. Because blackness carries within it the hallmarks of subjection, subalternity, and nonsovereignty, black subjects cannot appear under the rubrics—whether ideological, political, juridical, or cultural—of agentive, a priori personhood.[31] Moving beyond standard beliefs and practices of racial representation organized around identity, sentimentality, and inclusive politics, the artists who populate this study take a more radical and visionary approach to the production of black literature and art. I track the emergence of distinct aesthetic practices, the demolition or renovation of form and genre in black cultural production via the deployment of these aesthetic practices, and their unique instantiations of durable black life and radical political possibility. This book joins an emerging cadre of recent scholarly texts that analyze experimental black expressive formations, which are radically redefining and reorienting the field of African American literary and cultural studies.[32] Whether theorizing postblack or postsoul aesthetics, black subjectivity and sociality unencumbered by the injurious past of racial slavery, or the speculative and fantastical orientations of black literary and cinematic futures, this recent criticism turns toward the liberative possibilities of black experiment.[33] I refine and advance such field-altering work by distilling the black avant-garde into specific experimental modalities—Black Grotesquerie, Hollowed Blackness, Black Cacophony, and the Black Ecstatic—that have become, I argue, most preeminent and pervasive. In the chapters to follow, I explore each expressive modality in detail, pairing different expressive forms, such as, fiction and sculpture, poetry and cinema, digital exhibit and memoir, to study the work of cultural practitioners across the African diaspora.

Adducing black feminism's theories of the flesh and Mikhail Bakhtin's conception of the grotesque, chapter 1, "Black Grotesquerie," reads together Kenyan American visual artist Wangechi Mutu and African American genderqueer author Marci Blackman to make the case for Black Grotesquerie as an expressive mode that undermines the prevailing social order by confounding its representational logics. Black Grotesquerie reconfigures the terms of contemporary black struggle by rendering the boundary between (black) living and (black) dying porous and negotiable. As an expressive practice, it infuses the materiality of the black body with the textuality of the art object.

The acceptance of catastrophe as the context for black being, the practice of living on in outmoded shapes, the appetite for the unbearable underside of enjoyment, the determination to make last what has already been ruined—all are the signal features of Black Grotesquerie. Rather than merely signifying excess, dread, or decay, Black Grotesquerie delineates an aesthetic practice of contortion, exaggeration, substitution, inversion, corruption. As such, it is an expressive practice of formal disintegration and recombinant gathering—the assembly and aestheticization of remains—to open pathways for as-yet-unrealized and as-yet-unimagined black futures.

The second chapter, "Hollowed Blackness," pursues an investigation of racial confinement and affect via attention to Black Hollows and the black subjects who move into; sequester, enfold, or hide themselves in; or emerge, burst forth, or arise from them. By *Black Hollows / Hollowed Blackness*, I refer to (1) the material perimeters of caverns, ditches, basements, closets, attics that sometimes serve as sites of escape, momentary relief, or passage for black people fleeing racial and gendered horror and (2) the emotional state of hollowness that indicates black shock, emptiness, fatigue, doneness. Building on Katherine McKittrick's theorization of the "garreted" enslaved person in flight alongside Kevin Quashie's mandate that black studies attend to quiet black interiors, I read together the visual art of Alexandria Smith, the poetry of Aja Monet, and the fiction of Colson Whitehead. Taking seriously the ways in which racialized and gendered systems of captivity and control (from the plantation to the checkpoint to the prison) operate through the tyranny of compulsory visibility—that is, through techniques and technologies of ubiquitous surveillance, tracking, disclosure, and capture—this chapter rethinks abolitionism and reconsiders the spatial terrains of black freedom. Foregrounding the movements and maneuvers of the most terrorized and aggrieved black subjects, this chapter ultimately redirects the critical site of fugitivity from (the expanse of) the outdoors to (the interstitial zone of) the hollow.

Putting forth a theory of black sonic radicality and resistance, chapter 3, "Black Cacophony," examines depictions of screaming, howling, blabbering, moaning in both canonical and avant-garde black expressive texts. In so doing, it develops a theory of *Black Cacophony* as an aesthetic of noise *within* language, at its limits. My analysis proceeds from the premise that, for New World black subjects descended from the middle passage, what remains of and replaces a narrative of origins is a legacy of indecipherable sounds—or what Junot Díaz calls "the screams of the enslaved," and Toni Morrison calls their "roaring."[34] Reading cacophonous moments in literary depictions of

New World slavery and its afterlives, this chapter pursues two critical objectives: first, to illuminate the ways in which dissonant, evocative sound registers the affective dimensions of black experience, while complicating racial epistemologies and conventional narratives of racial harm; second, to show how language, when divested of its primary purpose of communication, is objectified and made available for scrutiny and for imaginative design. At the edge of discourse, or in its exhaustion, are the sonic resonances of form. Black Cacophony is a technique of textual representation that marks the superfluity *and* the insufficiency of language for capturing exploited or discarded subaltern life while insisting, in its sentient soundings, that such life matters.

Finally, the fourth chapter, "The Black Ecstatic," proffers ecstasy as the site of queer of color desire, relational practice, and utopic possibility to develop what I call the *Black Ecstatic* as a hermeneutic for analyzing post–civil rights black queer expressive culture. As an affective and aesthetic practice, the Black Ecstatic eschews both the heroism of black pasts and the promise of liberated black futures in order to proffer new relational and representational modes in the ongoing catastrophe that constitutes black life in modernity. As an aesthetic modality that deploys the practices and poetics of structural ambiguity—or, to use Ernst Bloch's words, "experiments in demolition"—the Black Ecstatic reveals how the labors of loss may lead to undocumented spaces and unanticipated experiences of freedom.[35] Against the backdrop of civil rights retrenchment, the war on drugs, the AIDS crisis and the emergent US carceral state, this chapter analyzes the recent film *Moonlight* and the poetry of black gay writer and AIDS activist Essex Hemphill. In so doing, it shows how, across literary genres and media platforms, the Black Ecstatic instantiates formal innovations to black queer expressive forms and encourages willful exuberance as an affective disposition and relational ethic that enables black life and liberation in the catastrophic present.

Millennial Style emerges at a time of crisis, where crisis is indistinct from the ongoing conditions of everydayness. Its critical scaffolding embeds and builds upon queer of color critique, critical race theory, and black feminist politics to reckon with and to register the interrelatedness of aesthetic abstraction, social abjection, and the global reach of political terror in the current moment. In her monumental *Toward a Global Idea of Race*, Denise Ferreira da Silva construes blackness as a fundamentally (and fruitfully) nonsovereign life form that can neither instate nor instantiate itself within the discursive and representational frames of modern citizen-subjectivity. She explains:

> No matter how fluid, hybrid, or unbounded, when addressing a collectivity the racial has already inscribed as subaltern, the cultural acquires a descriptive sense that does not and cannot communicate interiority, as is the case with the nation, the historical signifier. It does not and cannot precisely because it remains fully within a scientific (anthropological) terrain of signification. As such, it reinforces the effects of signification of the racial: exterior determination. In short, it cannot institute a transparent (interior/temporal)—that is, self-determined—"I."[36]

Rather than lamenting blackness's representative impossibility within dominant discourse, juridical paradigms, and political schemas, da Silva recodes this inability as black queer trans insurgency vis-à-vis modern subjectivity. In "Hacking the Subject," a later essay, she extols "blackness's ability to disrupt the subject and the racial and gender-sexual forms that sustain it, without sacrificing the latter's capacity to expose the fundamentally violent core of modern thinking."[37] Blackness exposes the white supremacist foundations of entitled, white, normatively gendered, legal, patriarchal personhood. My methods in *Millennial Style* are inspired in part by da Silva's theorization of hacking as a hermeneutic for black study. She suggests: "Hacking here is de\composition, or a radical transformation (or imaging) that exposes, unsettles, and perverts form and formulae. . . . Hacking is a kind of reading, which is at once an imaging (in Benjamin's sense, in reference to the work done by the dialectical image) and a composition (as description of a creative act), but also recomposition of elements, in the sense the term has in alchemy."[38]

I want to emphasize da Silva's use of the word *alchemy* to register the reshaping, entwining, esoteric engagement between the imaginative texts in this book and my readings of them. I proceed by deploying a method of creative and speculative criticism. Retrieving into the dominant culture's discourse the abstract practices of those denied subjecthood, inheriting a murderous history and living in a murderous present, requires acts of deformation and of experiment as well. My writing throughout this book purposely employs experimental strategies, such as collage, lyricism, speculation. My doing so reflects my recognition and regard for black avant-gardist practice as powerfully resistant to interpretive capture and to absorptive disciplinary regimes. Rather than aim for definitive authority and interpretive closure, my analyses of experimental black texts open them up in wonder and in a quest for a critical language and scholarly praxis within which to illuminate the barely visible, nearly impossible horizons of black freedom that these texts imagine.

I am guided by and adherent to the artistic practices, subversive possibilities, and innovative political interventions found in contemporary African diasporic literature and visual art. By exploring how abstract aesthetic practices upend the predominance of political sentimentality and formal realism in African diasporic expressive culture, I illuminate the centrality of the avant-garde to political modes of storytelling and visual representation *and* to the undercurrent of racial politics in late twentieth- and twenty-first-century black cultural production of high experiment. My cumulative offering in *Millennial Style* is a promiscuous reading of the archive of African diasporic cultural production in the new century, a conception of black temporality that reckons truly with the continuities and intricacies of political terror, and an exploration of the black avant-garde—which commits radically, if nonspectacularly, to an improved world for the minoritized, the neglected, the abandoned, the exhausted, the annihilated, the black.

1

BLACK GROTESQUERIE

The lost and the dead are not altogether absent.
—JOSÉ ESTEBAN MUÑOZ

To degrade an object does not merely imply hurling it into the void of nonexistence, into absolute destruction, but to hurl it down to . . . the zone in which conception and new birth takes place.
—MIKHAIL BAKHTIN

We need a new language of abstraction to explain this horror.
—FRANK B. WILDERSON III

A SKETCH

Offered less to communicate the status of a gone thing than to instantiate a refusal, Marci Blackman's *Tradition* opens with the word "Dead."[1] Yet the person to whom the word putatively refers, Finest Coon, is not, in fact, dead. He hovers in a liminal space where dead bespeaks a psychic, social, civic, monetary, and metaphysical condition; the character, Mabel, who pronounces this death is actually the one who has returned Finest from its brink. In *Tradition*, life and death are contingent—not permanent, impermeable—states. "Dead" in *Tradition* is resisted forcefully, produced lovingly, massaged at once into being and again into something else. Moreover, dead is always already bound up with racial blackness, with black beings who persist in altered forms of diminished life. Tarrying then with the dead, Blackman's novel is ultimately less invested in making a political case on behalf of black life than in exploring the weary, and wearying, ways that black people *live on*.[2] Living on refers here to the persistence and permutations of life forms excluded from the proper domain of the living—or, even more plainly, to the actions of the (black) dead.[3]

I invoke this moment in Blackman's novel to introduce the aesthetic mode and political vision that, I argue, *Tradition* puts forth, and that this chapter takes up and conceptualizes as *Black Grotesquerie*. Adducing women of color feminism's theories of the flesh and building on Mikhail Bakhtin's conception of the grotesque, Black Grotesquerie marks in contemporary black cultural production the deployment of the grotesque as an expressive mode that undermines the prevailing social order by confounding its representational logics.[4] The concept reconfigures the terms of contemporary black struggle by rendering the boundary between (black) living and (black) dying as porous and negotiable. The acceptance of catastrophe as the context for black being, the practice of living on in outmoded shapes, the appetite for the unbearable underside of enjoyment, the determination to make last what has already been ruined are all signal features of Black Grotesquerie. As an expressive practice, Black Grotesquerie infuses the materiality of the black body with the textuality of the art object; rather than merely signifying excess, dread, or decay, it delineates an aesthetic practice of exaggeration, substitution, distortion, inversion, corruption. The refusal and rupture of form underwrite the Black Grotesque aesthetic. Thus, my conceptualization of this aesthetic mode attends more assiduously to disturbed form than it does to disturbing content per se.

My theorization builds on Bakhtinian conceptions of the grotesque, which differ substantially from predominant notions in both common and critical lexica. We typically think of the grotesque as absurdity, ugliness, monstrosity, and the term is generally used, accordingly, to describe phenomena, occurrences, behaviors, things in the world. Mikhail Bakhtin posits the degradation of form, however, as the central principle of the grotesque:

> To degrade is to bury, to sow, and to kill simultaneously, in order to bring forth something more and better. To degrade also means to concern oneself with the lower stratum of the body, the life of the belly

> and the reproductive organs; it therefore relates to acts of defecation and copulation, conception, pregnancy, and birth. Degradation digs a bodily grave for a new birth; it has not only a destructive, negative aspect, but also a regenerating one. To degrade an object does not imply merely hurling it into the void of nonexistence, into absolute destruction, but to hurl it down to the reproductive lower stratum, the zone in which conception and a new birth take place.[5]

Bakhtin allegorizes political critique through the deployment of grotesque aesthetics, which depend on the familiar cycles, contours, and capacities of human embodiment. The human body emblematizes the coextension of vitality and vulgarity, of destruction and regeneration, in both artistic practice and social organization.

Bakhtin's conception of the grotesque derives from the materiality and the revelry of the carnival, which is a mode of sociality that undermines and parodies established sociopolitical systems. In *Rabelais and His World*, a book-length study of the Renaissance French writer Francois Rabelais, Bakhtin explores the interaction among social practice, corporeal embodiment, and literary form. Importantly, his study of their interaction concerns primarily how each refuses fixity and stasis, overruns its structured boundaries, inverts and topples order, and challenges the assignation of value in hierarchized societal, political, and cosmological systems. "The suspension of all hierarchical precedence during carnival time was of particular significance," he specifies.[6] "All were considered equal during carnival. Here, in the town square, a special form of free and familiar contact reigned among people who were usually divided by the barriers of caste, property, profession, and age."[7] The festivity and ribaldry of the carnival reflect their orientation toward pleasure and profane excess. The carnival sanctions generalized unconventionality and the suspension of hegemony. The critical and political potential of the carnival lies in its spectacularization of a topsy-turvy social order, in which the ruling elite's right of control and command is momentarily dispossessed and turned inside out. More than a fixed property of aesthetic objects, then, the grotesque delineates a *process* and *a performance* of revaluing and repositioning the debased elements of bodily, structural, conceptual, and worldly configurations. The Black Grotesque discomfits the world, disarranging and reforming the official order of things.

In "Venus in Two Acts," Saidiya Hartman attempts to exhume and examine the presence of black women and girls in the textual and material traces of New World slavery. Hartman illuminates movingly the critical impasse, or impossibility, of locating narrativizable black life in the absent presences of destroyed black girls who, entombed in mere material residue, refuse reckoning and, thus, thwart the scholar's counterhistorical endeavor. Hartman cannot recuperate the millions of enslaved who enter the historical record under the names "Hottentot. A sulky bitch. A dead negress. A syphilitic whore," whose lives are indexed primarily by scribbled figures, lines, and numbers in ledgers that record quantified human value, rates of capitalist expansion, the multitude of black dead in the documented histories of transatlantic slavery.[8] For Hartman the intellectual and political stakes of her work in the archive are manifestly evident. To imagine modes of endurance for persons and populations born(e) out of *and yet into* the afterlives of slavery requires the historian's archaeological labor. Hartman serves as agent and conduit for irruptions of the horrific past of embodied black slavery into the discursive and social domains of the present. The project of freedom necessitates these encounters.

Nevertheless, the archives and the ongoing effects of subjective erasure produced by the legacies of colonial writing and (or as) accounting create problems of both suitable narrative form and suitable aesthetic mode. Recording black lives in the aftermath of modern regimes of racial bondage requires narrative techniques at the edge of discourse. There is, after all, no practice of recovery that negates all prior harm. "Venus in Two Acts" draws on the language of drama to demarcate the double failings that confront its stated aims: these failures are, first, the limits of what can ever be recovered or revealed about the ordinary, operative violences of New World slavery, and, second, the limits of historiography as methodology and metadiscourse for such recovery and revelation. Taken together, these limits engender a shift in Hartman's authorial position from that of scholar-historian to that of imaginative writer. Hartman writes the history of New World slavery by staging literary experiments, which she explains in terms of "flattening," "toppling," and "engulf[ing] authorized speech" in order to weave "present, past, and future in retelling the girl's story and in narrating the time of slavery as our present."[9] Hartman's narrative derangements simultaneously reflect and engender profound structural ambivalence, overlapping and disjunctive temporalities, semantic dissolution, and fantastical possibility. At once an essay, an elegy, a polemic, a play, and a lament, "Venus in Two Acts" proceeds through a rupture and refusal of form.

In its critical conception and artful enactment, Black Grotesquerie reflects black political desire for "something for which there is no coherent articulation."[10] It is an expressive practice of formal disintegration and recombinant gathering—the assembly and aestheticization of remains—that open pathways for as-yet-unrealized and as-yet-unimagined black futures.[11] Taking seriously black life as defined by the perpetuity of crisis, Black Grotesquerie promotes *living on* as the capacity of black people to be—that is, to exist and endure—in the ever-broken now. In what follows, I illustrate how Black Grotesquerie enables African diaspora cultural producers to imagine new sociopolitical and racial arrangements, even as this aesthetic mode registers the impossibility of fully representing black experience, whether in historical time *or* postracial futurity. By emphasizing the fallacy of postracialism that remains operant in our simultaneously neoliberal and neofascist times, I argue that the combined industries of the carceral system and welfare reform perpetuate conditions of abrogated—even wholly negated—citizenship for African Americans that recall and reenact modes of racial abjection inaugurated during New World slavery. The chapter unfolds to advance the argument that in the twenty-first century racialized abjection defines the condition of proximal black living, slow death, and group demise. Furthermore, I illustrate the failure of traditional black representational modes under current conditions of perpetual, if not permanent, containment and disposal. Foregrounding black feminist theories of the flesh, the chapter proceeds to explore the linkage between racialized abjection and Black Grotesquerie as an aesthetic mode, incorporating an analysis of three works by multimedia visual artist Wangechi Mutu. The chapter concludes with a return to Blackman's *Tradition* as an exemplar of Black Grotesquerie in new millennial African American fiction. Ultimately, what this chapter demonstrates is how, across visual and literary texts, Black Grotesquerie operates as a new millennial aesthetic of ironic capture, where what may be found by looking closely and closer still are undocumented spaces of freedom, the barest repair, and private joy in the continuous, catastrophic present.

THE CATASTROPHIC PRESENT

We are living in the future tense of abolition; decolonization; integration; first-, second-, and third-wave feminism; and black power, yet contemporary black life remains mired in regressive, recursive time.[12] This new millennial, neoliberal moment evinces what Jared Sexton cogently characterizes as "a historical continuum . . . not cessation or interruption of historical flow but persistence of historical force, persistence in and as permutation."[13] The problem of racism, its stratification of human life, and its undoing of black potential was supposedly remedied by the legislative rights and protections secured during the civil rights movement. Those legislative gains of the mid-twentieth century are believed to have eradicated the last vestiges of racism in the United States. Not long ago, however, Kimberlé Crenshaw thought it important to remind an audience at Harvard University that the "continuation of dramatic disparities across race along almost every conceivable measure renders the claim that race has lost its social legibility rather dubious. It is neither by chance nor by stereotype that one can assign life status, occupation, income and mortality by race in the U.S."[14] As had been made painfully evident by the inauguration of the Trump era and its aftermath, the decades since the legislative triumphs of the civil rights movement have been marked by the steady retraction of gains: the abrogation of the most enshrined rights for minoritized, gendered subjects and the curtailment of the most basic civil liberties; the hypersurveillance and hypermilitarization of urban spaces and national borders; obscene and ever-widening economic disparities; and the rampant denial of the ordinary protections and provisions of sustainable life to black and brown populations globally.

In this country, race continues to determine disparate individual and group outcomes and to function as the central mechanism by which rights and resources are asymmetrically allocated and withheld. The dream of racial equality, rhetorically and symbolically indexed by whether an embodied black man could be US president, has been fulfilled.[15] Still, as Colin Dayan notes, "the continued criminalization of African Americans in this country is what drives our nation—legally, politically, and socially. That a city has elected a black mayor, a country a black president, changes nothing for many of our fellow citizens who face casual cruelty and enduring harm simply because they are black."[16] Instead of instituting policies to alleviate the lethal impacts of material and sociopolitical exclusion on marginalized, minoritized populations, successive US presidencies over the twenty-first century have continued to extend what Dylan Rodriguez describes as the American state's "undeclared/domestic warfare" against impoverished communities comprised primarily of people of color, whom it targets for "social liquidation and/or political neutralization."[17] Moreover, the system of social services and social supports—particularly agencies designed to support distressed families and communities like Departments of Transitional Assistance for Needy Families and Child Protective Services—aligns with the carceral industry as a technology of civil rights retraction effected through the criminalization of racialized populations. The exponential growth of the prison industrial complex exacerbates the structural dismantling of the rights and protections secured by African Americans through legislation.[18] The so-called war on drugs of the 1980s, along with mandatory sentencing laws (that led, in some cases, to lifetime imprisonment for crimes as insignificant as buying and selling marijuana), the disenfranchisement of over one million African Americans attributed to felony convictions and the expansive development and concurrent privatization of the US carceral industry has led to the unabated disproportionate mass incarceration of black subjects of *all genders* throughout and beyond Barack Obama's presidency.[19] The fact of continued black suffering and exacerbated group demise both during and following the era of black presidential leadership bespeaks the intractability of antiblack racism in Western world-making.

The recursive temporality of transatlantic slavery manifests specifically in the interlocking industries of racial containment and racial capitalism. Since the 1970s the prison population has grown over 700 percent, with African American men, women, and youth primarily targeted, mishandled, profiled, convicted, sentenced, contained, immobilized—often in isolation, sometimes for life, if they are not shot dead prior to or during an arrest.[20] Taken together, the prison industrial complex and the welfare system fundamentally normalize the status and affiliated conditions negating citizenship for African Americans that began under New World slavery. According to Dennis Childs, "Formations of chattel slavery have resurfaced in updated forms in the context of a system of mass civil, premature/living death, and human incapacitation . . . which entombs more than 2.3 million human beings and, more specifically, a modern penitentiary system that now encages one out of every nine black men in the United States between the ages of twenty and twenty-nine."[21] The modern penitentiary operates through the capture, confinement, and incapacitation of black subjects en masse. In so doing, it may be understood as the structured, site-specific logic and operation of white supremacy. White supremacist regimes, according to Dylan Rodriguez, "from racial chattel slavery and frontier genocide to recent and current modes of land displacement and (domestic/undeclared) warfare—are sociologically entangled with the state's changing paradigms, strategies, and technologies of human incarceration and punishment."[22] Rather than inhabiting a dream of postracial equality that evinces the final triumph of the United States over its legacies of racial slavery, contemporary black life is subject to a regime of protoslavery in which the political disenfranchisement and social disposability of racialized populations remain the cornerstones of the national economy.[23] I spend some time here detailing the ongoing political and carceral procedures by which black subjects are steadily converted into the socially disenabled and politically discarded in order to underscore the importance of Black Grotesquerie as an artistic mode in the face of racism's intractable force. Textually and materially, Black Grotesquerie rehabilitates incapacitated black life: it deploys such techniques as corruption, inversion, contortion, and substitution to aesthetically and ethically recover the wretched.

IMAG(IN)ING THE BLACK GROTESQUE

As an aesthetic practice, Black Grotesquerie transgresses and transforms the boundaries among social organization, embodied life, and cultural production. As both an innovative aesthetic practice and a strategic mode of signification, it captures potently racialized abjection in contemporary expressive culture of the African diaspora. By *racialized abjection*, I mean both the structural harms outlined in the section above and the manifold experiences of degradation that assail embodied black people as we exist and circulate in the world.[24] Black Grotesquerie is deployed in new millennial African diaspora expressive culture to foreground phenomena and experiences of debasement as potential sources of regenerative capacity. Fundamentally animated by the (nonnarrativizable) knowledge of abbreviated life, incapacitated life, premature death, and living death, it alters the terms and reconfigures the boundary between (black) living and dying. As contemporary black life is suspended between polarities of death (whether civic, social, or corporeal), the Black Grotesque principle of *living on* is both aesthetically and politically resonant for postslavery black subjects, whom Abdul Jan Mohamed calls "death-bound."[25]

Like literary practitioners, world-renowned visionary Kenyan American multimedia visual artist Wangechi Mutu deploys Black Grotesque aesthetics to rescue black futurity from the irremediable past. She does so in part by incorporating and subverting racial caricatures that were widely disseminated in nineteenth-century Euro-American pseudosciences, popular media, and commodity culture. Centered on the historical implications of New World slavery and the apocalyptic implications of genocidal warfare in the twentieth and twenty-first centuries, Mutu's *Howl* presents cyborgian para/sub/humans produced through recombinant multimedia collage techniques (figure 1.1). *Howl* registers a mode of living on, a form of life that barely is.

The African continent, divvied up and pillaged, is inscribed in the tiny shard of bleeding earth to which one abject figure clings and from which two others fall. Embodying the despair of the remnant—simultaneously what is left over and who is left behind—after racial slavery, colonial occupation, and genocide, Mutu's cyborgian para/sub/humans claw, scrape, holler, barely hold

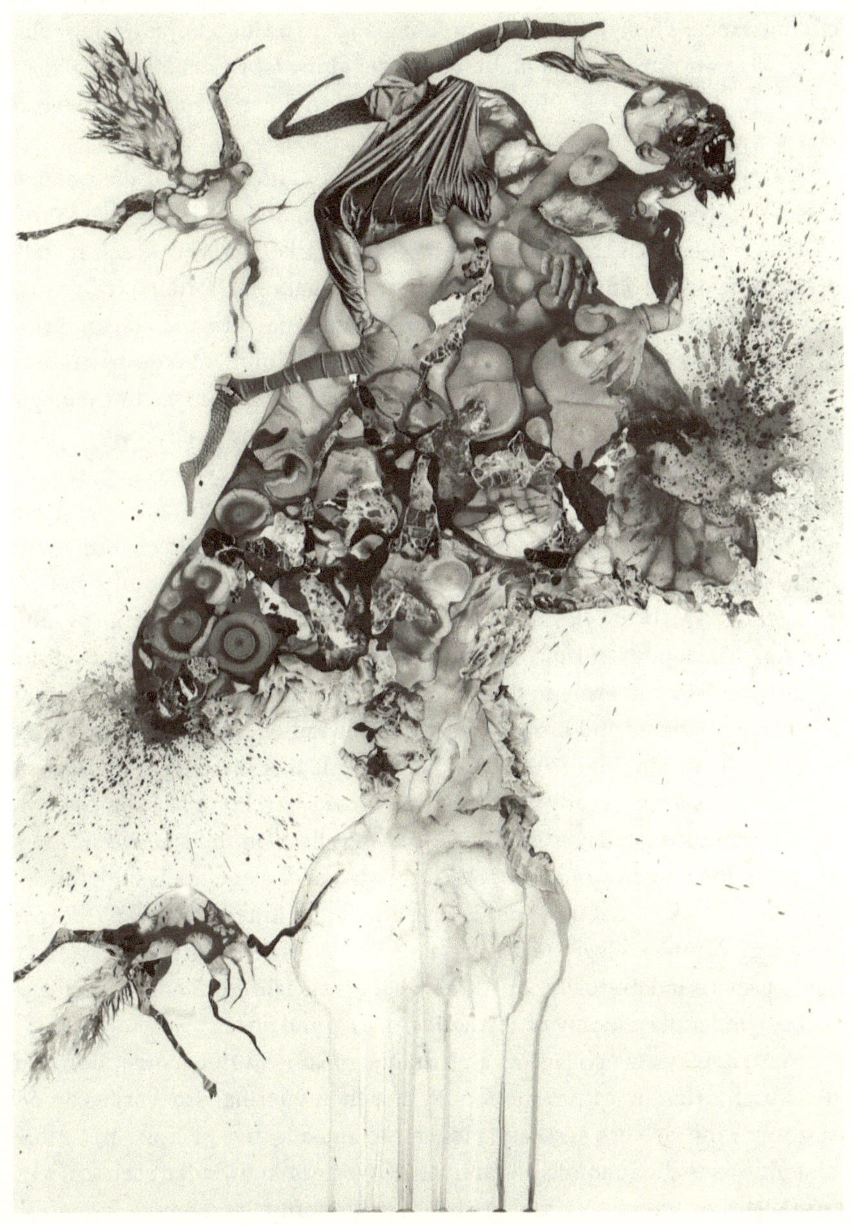

FIGURE 1.1 Wangechi Mutu, *Howl*, 2006. Ink, collage, and mixed media on Mylar, 35 × 24 in. Courtesy of the artist and Vielmetter Los Angeles.

on. The overlap of textures and items besets the notion of history as a past occurrence that might provide the causal and temporal logic for the present circumstance. Though they seem at first glance to be insect eyes, fashionable sunglasses are worn by the main figure; her shiny fabrics cling to her form. As her mutilated legs scatter like so many windblown branches, the figure appears anguished in the midst of mutation.

A symbol of geopolitical, material, cultural, and temporal dissonance, the cyborgian para/sub/human—whom we might call simply the *female black*—is the product of the current world-market system, which installs racial and socioeconomic asymmetries across national borders, (re)creates slave labor conditions to facilitate the mass manufacture and consumption of superfluous commodities, and hastens the environmental destruction of our shared world. The abstract ideal of the human originates in the negation of the female black, given shape in Mutu's *Howl* as the cyborgian para/sub/human. Victims of a murderous modernity, Mutu's cyborgian para/sub/humans conjure the countless labors and horrors to which captive and colonized female blacks have been subject. Hartman has adroitly summarized these as "converted into cash, speculated and traded as commodity, worked to death, taken, tortured, seeded, and propagated like any other crop, or murdered."[26] The figures in *Howl* do not merely indicate the plight of black dislocation and dismemberment; they interrogate the abstract ideal of the human as the paradigmatic and proper rights-entitled entity. Instead of augmenting unitary perception, Mutu's multimedia image further disarranges that which the collage as form already undermines. As Zakiyyah Iman Jackson cogently explains: "Mutu's collages invite viewers to reflect on their aesthetic judgments as the perceived harmony or discordance of elements is undergirded by historically situated taxonomies and typologies (often scientific). More to the point, Mutu's collages reveal the extent to which Western science and visual art share and mutually constitute what is a racialized, gendered, and sexualized imperial economy of aesthetics, desire, and affect."[27]

Mutu deploys the collage as a technique of substitution, corruption, and denaturalization in art production. Rather than offering visual art as an occasion for the viewer's aesthetic judgement and affective pleasure in a mode that affirms the taxonomic hierarchies of Western knowledge regimes, Mutu's collage techniques disrupt the affective sensorium and render indivisible the specist-racist ordering of Man. *Howl* is a collage that screams, not only disorganizing visual phenomena—which are already disparate, fractured, and temporally disjunctive—but also altering the expected muteness of the object. The red paint splatter in *Howl* visually represents both the blood wound of collectivized black trauma and the amplification of the *animate* object's (i.e., the slave or the para/sub/human's)(out)cry. Beyond merely embodying a disposable form of life, the figures in *Howl* capture, in the shape of African diasporic female subjectivity, the catastrophic trajectory of Euro-American modernity.

The afterlives and aftereffects of imperial domination are traceable in the planetary displacement of populations, failed national sovereignties, ecological ruination, and innumerable humanitarian disasters that have already occurred in the twenty-first century. For Ann Stoler, "duress" articulates the somatic affect, protracted temporality, and hazardous residues of colonial legacies in the present. Stoler underscores the shared etymological root of duress, duration and durability in search of a promise, asserting that "*endurance* figures here, as well, in the capacity to 'hold out' and 'last,' especially in its activated form, 'to endure' as a countermand to 'duress' and its damaging and disabling qualities."[28] Moving beyond the understanding of duress as the physical and psychic experience of one's own wearying waste (of time, of human potential), she arrives at endurance: the practice of living on, of outliving simultaneously one's assigned function and its failure. She asserts:

> Duress, then, is neither a thing nor an organizing principle so much as a relation to a condition, a pressure exerted, a troubled condition borne in the body, a force exercised on muscles and mind. It may bear no immediately visible sign, or alternatively, it may manifest in a weakened constitution or attenuated capacity to bear its weight. Duress is tethered to time but rarely in a predictable way. It may be a response to relentless force, to the quickened pacing of pressure, to intensified or arbitrary inflictions that reduce expectations and stamina. Duress rarely calls out its name. Often, it is a mute condition of restraint. Legally it does something else. To claim to be "under duress" in a court of law does not absolve one of a crime or exonerate the fact of one. On the contrary, it admits a culpability—a condition induced by illegitimate pressure. But it is productive, too, of a diminished burned-out will not to succumb, when one is stripped of the wherewithal to have acted differently or better.[29]

Duress bespeaks the physical and emotional difficulty of wearing out, "in muscle and mind," in response to repetitive enactments and experiences of subjugation. As mortal and material resources disappear under relentless or renewed occupation of the colony and postcolony, duress comes to define the individuated and collectivized reality of living within the logics, geographies, and legacies of imperialist domination. Nevertheless, embedded conceptually within duress (as both its peril and its promise) is that as harm endures, so, too, do its subjects. Stoler's invocation of the law and the one who breaks it under duress conveys the subversiveness of living on as the refusal to succumb. In both etymology and eventuality, duress and endurance are tethered via criminal continuance: what was supposed to die (or die out) instead perseveres. Endurance names the phenomenon and lived enactments of African diasporic subjects who, despite their clearly withered stamina and manifest—if, at times, mute—brokenness, recompose themselves and reconfigure the wretchedness of antiblack racism and material deprivation to keep on keeping on. Black Grotesquerie shows up in Wangechi Mutu's work as the aestheticized internalization of what has been ruined and the interiorization of what has been lost that illustrate how female blacks *somehow* keep on keeping on.

Notably, I am not the first viewer critic to examine the grotesque features of Mutu's art praxis. For example, in a published interview with Wangechi Mutu, Tiffany E. Barber and Angela Naimou reflect on her contribution to the 2015 Venice Biennale, writing that her work provides "insight into the relationship between art, artists, and the pervasive disorder that structures contemporary social life. This disorder is often allegorized in the figures that populate Mutu's recent art, which features phantasmagoric spaces replete with *nguva* (the Kiswahili word for sirens and mermaids), serpents, and other otherworldly creatures."[30] Reflecting on Mutu's ambivalent portrayals of black women's erotic subjectivities, primarily through the hybridization of pornographic and ethnographic print images in her collages, Jillian Hernandez describes her work as "exhibit[ing] the boundary-crossing and combinatory elements of the grotesque."[31] My invocation of grotesquerie to describe both the design and method of Mutu's multimedia art installations reflects a shared concern with these critics of her work's ambiguity, otherworldliness, and disordered assembly. Nevertheless, by emphasizing specifically the Bakhtinian conception of grotesquerie as the regeneration of the dead(ened) and the renewal of the degraded, I am reaching for what Mutu's aesthetic practice might reveal about black living and, particularly, about black living on in the current moment.

In their formal composition, Mutu's Black Grotesque renderings of collaged multimedia visual art unfinish the past and unmake what is given by (re)presenting the racially abject body as a fluctuating surface. Black feminist scholars theorize the flesh as the site of ontological human (in effect, racial) differentiation, as the epistemological groundwork for Enlightenment theories of the relationship between personhood and possession, and as the primary form of New World currency.[32] The distinctions in what Sylvia Wynter terms "the genres of the human" are made and unmade at the level of skin and bone, rooted in the world-historical economic and ideological arrangement in which certain bodies could be—and were—made to move and act and reproduce and suffer and labor and die under the force and on behalf of another's motive.[33] Hortense Spillers centers the dispossessed corporeality of the black body, particularly in its rupture and ruin ("eyes beaten out; arms, backs, skulls branded; a left jaw, a right ankle punctured; missing teeth") to describe the historico-political circumstance of African diasporic subjects. She contends: "The body whose flesh carries the female and the male to the frontiers of survival bears in person the marks of a cultural text whose inside has been turned outside."[34] Invoking the figure of the enslaved black woman and deploying the trope of reproduction, Spillers (re)casts the human as a cultural text, suggesting that strategies of black survival depend on embodied conceptions of the human, *of the nonsovereign subject*—which, when disarticulated from Western man, exceeds the containments of surface and skin.[35] Even as Black Grotesquerie inscribes racialized abjection in the ruptures of bone and flesh, it challenges the belief that the body is the site where identities are formed and affixed. We encounter the beginnings of Hartman's counterhistory of the human in the grotesque principle of inversion, or what Spillers calls the cultural text whose inside has been turned outside.

The exhibit of Wangechi Mutu's *Sentinel I* and *Sentinel II* presents the sculptural figures as paired. Mutu, now living in and working between Nairobi and New York, shipped the pieces across the Atlantic to be featured in the 2019 Whitney Biennial. The installation thus reenacted the inherent perils and vexed possibilities of transatlantic crossings for African-descended subjects: the longing and labor of the migrant, the unmaking and monetization of the enslaved, the risk and relief of the refugee. My analysis here focuses specifically on *Sentinel II*, even as (or because) I recognize that the sentinel—as guard or soldier who is tasked with looking or watching out for the group—implies multiplicity, relationality, and reciprocity (figure 1.2). The installation visualizes and sculpturally instantiates the human as nonsovereign subject. The humanized, humanoid figure of *Sentinel II* is materially and ontologically earthy. Cast as an ecological assemblage, it is made of concrete, wood, gourd, and stone, among other materials. The folds of its design and of its dress are hardened earth. At once a statue, a sculpture, a sentinel, at over seven feet tall, *Sentinel II* is imposing, its elaborate and elegant headdress suggestive of high fashion, high royalty, and high military rank. Mutu's sculpture

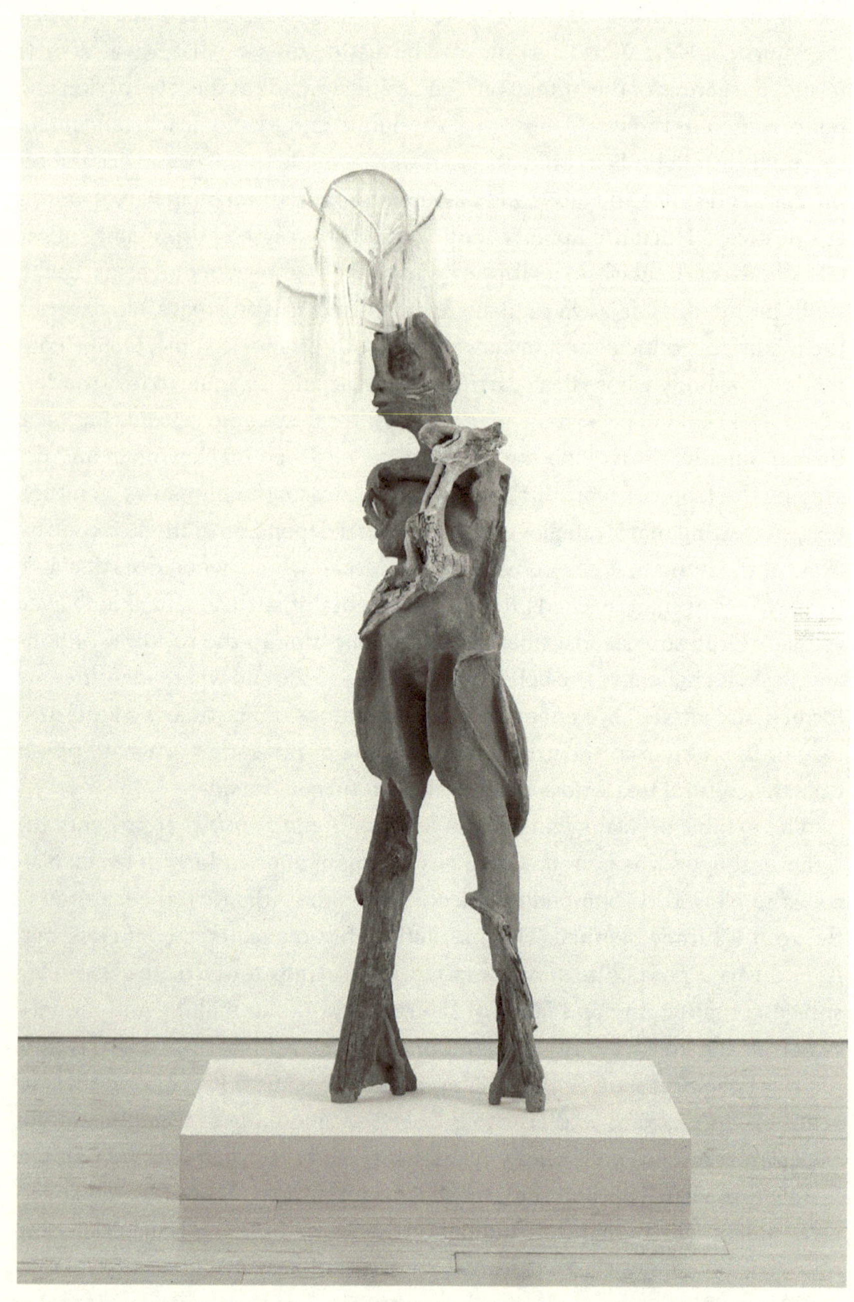

FIGURE 1.2 Wangechi Mutu, *Sentinel II*, 2018. Red soil, pulp, wood glue, concrete, wood, beads, stones, rose quartz, bone, and acrylic hair, 79⅛ × 20⅞ × 22 in. Courtesy of the artist and Gladstone Gallery. Photo credit: David Regen.

is as striking for what it presents as for what it is missing: arms, hands, the same two feet. In this installation, mutilation—wood-pierced breast, severed limbs—intimates the violences of resource extraction, geographic dislocation, and killing labor on the African continent.

We might, then, think of *Sentinel II* as a figural, three-dimensional map of and to African diasporic futures, with the figure embodying black time as recurrent and resurgent.[36] As its composite materials commingle what has passed with what is to come, *Sentinel II* summons primordial imprints for a future that is likely to be more ruinous than reparative. The various elements that comprise the sculpture shape and sustain habitats, nourishment, adornment, all here rescued, refinished, repurposed. Though seemingly anatomically female, I want to suggest that *Sentinel II* appears along a continuum of gender and a continuum of species. The stillness of the figure's stance—feet (or hooves) rooted and pointed forward, legs minimally but firmly apart—captures the inanimacy of the mannequin, the survival instincts of the para/sub/human, the intransigence of the militant. In every sense a molecular and modal pastiche, *Sentinel II* performs the artistic arrest, a ceasing, of the conjoined downward spirals of bodily disintegration and social debilitation, to which black subjects the world over are susceptible, via ecological innovation and formal hybridization.

While making a claim neither for artistic intent nor for explicit referentiality, my analysis discovers in Mutu's *Blue Rose* the beautification of Emmett Till's opened face (figure 1.3), notably going against the grain of most studies of Wangechi Mutu's art practice in that it does not tout exclusively feminized representation. By attending to the histories of black gruesome demise as they impact black subjects across genders and, within the visual repertoires of black political protest, wed black masculine loss to black maternal grief, I underscore the dismantling and mutability of black genders in order to investigate the complicated workings of racialized (un)gender in Mutu's Black Grotesque art practice. My reading refers to the widely circulated and widely referenced photograph of Emmett Till in his coffin. Lynched for allegedly whistling (or saying, "Bye, baby") to a white woman, Till was a most beautiful fourteen-year-old boy—before the white men took him away, beat him, shot him, severed his right eye from its socket, tied a seventy-pound fan around his neck, and left him submerged in the Tallahatchie River.[37] At his funeral, his mother, Mamie Till Bradley, insisted "that her son's face be seen, be shown, that his death and her mourning be performed. His face was destroyed," Moten writes. "It was turned inside out, ruptured, exploded, but more than that it was opened."[38] Moten theorizes the scene and the sight

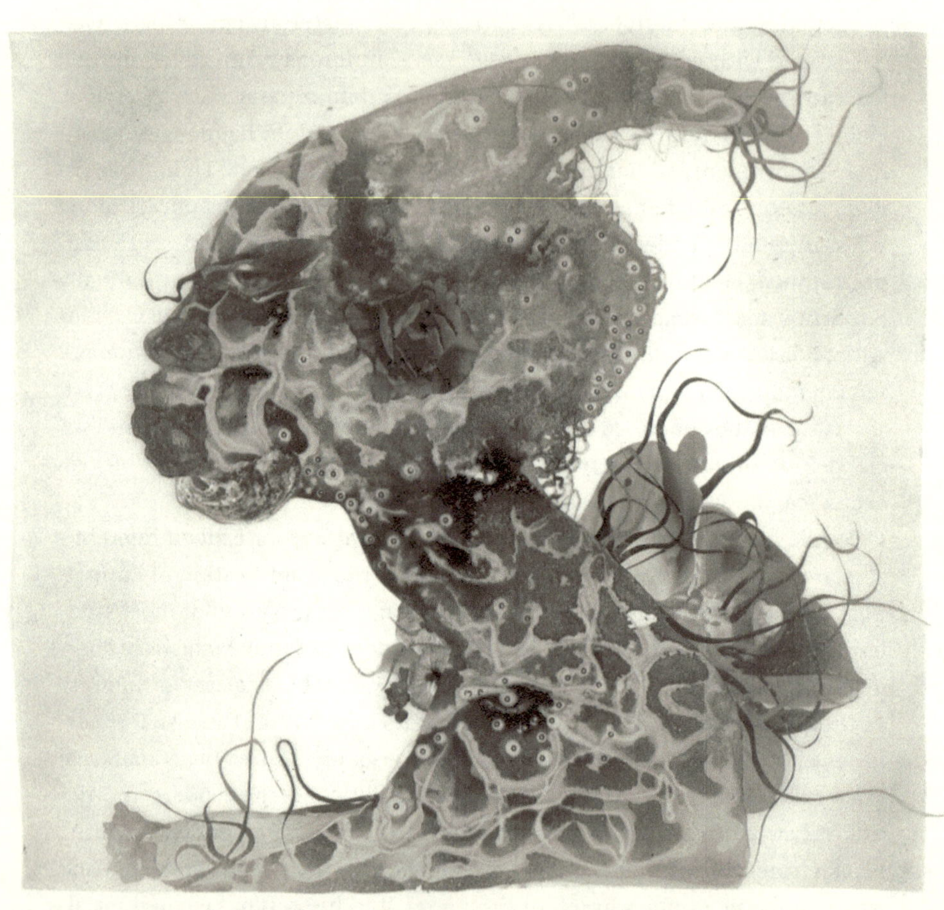

FIGURE 1.3 Wangechi Mutu, *Blue Rose*, 2007. Ink, collage, plant materials, and plastic pearls on Mylar, 53 × 87 in. Courtesy of the artist and Victoria Miro Gallery.

of Emmett Till's face as an individual, distilled—if by no means exclusive or exceptional—expression of lynching's particular horror. Ritual lynching was a mode of racial control implemented through the opening of black bodies to spectacular demise and terroristic viewing. Even as Mamie Till-Bradley mobilized lynching's horrifying optics to decry the gruesome murder of her child, Mutu subverts such optics.

In Mutu's work, as within Black Grotesque aesthetic practice generally, racialized bodies are in constant flux. As forms, they are neither fragmented nor fixed. Notably, the fluctuations in/of form connote racialized modes of living on in altered, if disintegrated, (non- or sub-) human shapes. In *Blue Rose*, which depicts a bust, an honored form of memorialization, black masculine gender and sexuality are fused with what seems to be an ungendered drowned face, still living. This graphic fusion reflects and powerfully resignifies *via symbolic coronation* the legendary hypersexuality of the black, which was touted as the predominant justification for lynching and its bloody decimation of black men in particular. Notably, when Till was pulled from the water, an eye and ear were missing. Mutu's mixed-media painting embeds plants and plastic pearls in the oceanic bust, with blue roses blooming out of the vacant crevices of the water-distorted face. As this image invokes in my reading Emmett Till's initial watery grave, it also serves as a monument to those enslaved Africans who died in the Middle Passage and to those stateless African subjects who die now in perilous flight from homes ravaged by the aftereffects of colonialism.[39] The figure in *Blue Rose*, as in Mutu's work in general, is shown to inhabit the interstitial states between living and dying *by virtue* of its contortions, distortions, protrusions. The embedded pearls, flowered orifices, and molecular texture endow the figure with a treasured vitality that imputes value and insinuates persistence beyond the violences that subtend and produce mass black death. Mutu deploys Black Grotesquerie to vitalize otherwise inert abstractions.

OF BLACK GROTESQUE FICTION . . . AND FINEST

Our new millennial present is characterized by the evident failure of racial equality during the first US black presidency and the rise of resurgent, fascistic, white supremacist leadership in the subsequent presidency. Black Grotesquerie has emerged as an important aesthetic mode among African American writers in times of heightened political disappointment and racial terror. Its techniques are evident in many recent black works of fiction: for example, in Carolivia Herron's 1991 experimental and sweeping apocalyptic novel of black intergenerational incest, *Thereafter Johnnie*; in Octavia Butler's 2005 novel of vampire genealogies and regeneration, *Fledgling*; in Alice Randall's 2009 *Rebel Yell*, which attempts to come to terms with a black neocon who participates in Confederate Civil War reenactments and eventually dies at one of them. *Rebel Yell* devotes its first quarter, about one hundred pages, to descriptions of the neocon's death and the disposal of his corpse. Sapphire's 2011 novel, *The Kid*, similarly models a Black Grotesque text. A follow-up to the harrowing *Push*, *The Kid* is a tale of manifold abuses endured *and committed* by an adolescent black boy who moves through various stages and sites of state custody as the result of a clerical error that fails to place him with loving relatives. Each of these texts probes what might be saved (or savored) in every scene of loss, in every act of historical violation.

In its production of shattering, its refusal of form, its embrace of ruin, its tactic of bare living on, Black Grotesquerie departs from realist narratives of individual and collective racial ruin. As an expressive mode, the grotesque undoes social hierarchies not through reversals based on totalized negation but through the integration of dichotomous processes oriented fundamentally toward "universal renewal."[40] The integration of dichotomous processes is captured in the aforementioned novels via formal techniques of narrative experiment. In their study of the grotesque in film and literature, Justin D. Edwards and Rune Grauland argue that the subversive impact of grotesquerie obtains in its challenge to "the limits of conventional aesthetics through disharmony or experimental forms."[41] In our present, defined by the perpetuity of crisis, literary practitioners of Black grotesquerie politicize literary form *by refusing* to stabilize it as externally referential or internally coherent.

Marci Blackman's breathtaking novel *Tradition* illustrates powerfully the deployment of Black Grotesquerie in new millennial African American writing. A multilayered, temporally overlapping, polyvocal text of alternating familial salvation and demise over the long sweep of a century, *Tradition* cuts and roams among three periods: the Depression era, the aftermath of World War II, and the year of Barack Obama's first presidential campaign. The novel is most invested in temporal surrounds, overstepping what might be regarded as the causal or culminating occurrence—the central event from which all action proceeds or around which it might all eventually cohere—and vacillating instead between preliminary moments of hope and possibility and histories that haunt and hurt. The novel opens in the year 2007, with the elderly Gus Weesfree returning to his childhood home after decades. As the novel moves between different epochs, the entangled stories of the Weesfree family unfold through brief, disjunctive scenes portraying the novel's multiple protagonists.

The family patronym Weesfree is a play on the phrase "We's free," an ironic pun capturing the African American dream of equitable citizenship and unqualified civic inclusion at the dawn of two new centuries: first, in the early twentieth century, during the Great Migration, and, second, in the early twenty-first century, on the cusp of Obama's election. As all of its central characters are either elderly or dead, the novel chronicles the slow demise of collective black life and of the traditional practices of black survival and social advancement. In 2007, the town, accessible by a road called the Bone, is overrun by bulldozers. As the environment outside of the Weesfree family home is being demolished, its insides are also disintegrating. The text describes in exquisite detail the decrepit furniture and shabby walls; Gus's sister Mabel's aging, alcoholic body; and Gus's best friend, the sedentary and severely disfigured Finest Coon, who is falling literally apart.

The novel portrays numerous types of *common* abuse: child abuse, the abuse of the disabled, veteran abuse, police and government abuse, spousal abuse, and the sexual abuse of motherless children. The novel depicts women dying in childbirth and from heartbreak. It represents patricide alternately as an act of revenge and as an act of mercy. The aesthetics of the grotesque are evident in the ambivalent portrayals of all these occurrences. As my conception of Black Grotesquerie builds on the Bakhtinian grotesque, my reading of Blackman's novel foregrounds the generally degraded and occluded sites of the body. Of the grotesque body, Bakhtin writes:

> It is not a closed, completed unit; it is unfinished, outgrows itself, transgresses its own limits. The stress is laid on those parts of the body that are open to the outside world, that is, the parts through which the world enters the body or emerges from it, or through which the body itself goes out to meet the world. This means that the emphasis is on the apertures or the convexities, or on various ramifications and offshoots: the open mouth, the genital organs, the breasts, the phallus, the potbelly, the nose.[42]

The orifices and apertures of the body as well as its protrusive and penetrative features metonymize its capacities for the production and preservation of life: inhalation, exhalation, ingestion, elimination, consumption, excretion, reproduction, enunciation. The zones of the body typically associated with debasement, shame, vulnerability—what Bakhtin calls the "lower stratum"—are the anatomical sites where the vitality of animate matter is sustained and at times (re)made anew.[43] It is important to underscore here that, even as he emphasizes bodily nourishment, preservation, reproduction, and renewal in his revaluation of corporeal zones, Bakhtin's concern is nonetheless with the wider social body. Via upturning and inverting hierarchies of order and value, grotesquerie centers degraded, excluded populations and exalts them.

As a narrative technique, Black Grotesquerie pervades *Tradition*. Its features are most evident in the central character, Finest Coon, a mutilated African American veteran. Described as a ghostly man, Finest Coon spends most of his time handcuffed to furniture, sweating profusely, watching TV, and occasionally urinating on himself. Moreover, Finest Coon is a figure of racialized ungendering, as he is associated primarily with the lower sphere of the body: the reproductive, genital, and excretory region.[44] His severe facial deformity reflects that association: his "nose [s]mashed into his face like a mound of soft clay punched flat with the knuckles on a fist. His moustache and his lip squished up against the leveled bridge of his nose, at his chin welded into his mouth and jawbones like metals with no business being fused, and . . . his scars. Twitching."[45] Similar to Mutu's figures, Finest Coon's face is genitalized through terms reminiscent of the ways that black women's faces were represented in late nineteenth-century pseudoscientific and sexological discourses.[46] The violence that produced Finest's facial disfigurement resonates in the language used to describe it. No longer a phallic protrusion, his nose has been flattened into the common metaphor for the vagina: a mound. The damage and deterioration of Finest's visage permanently links him to the abject black maternal body.[47] Finest's head was misshaped during his torturous exit through his dying mother's birth canal, and he was further damaged by burns as a teenager after setting on fire his family home, with his father dead inside, killed by Finest after years of sexual torment. The elder Coon repeatedly dressed his son in his dead mother's clothes and, while taunting the boy for both his mother's death and his alleged ugliness, masturbated in front of him. Incest and pedophilia are here enacted via inappropriate and intrusive gazing, by looking at and touching what lies beneath.

Significantly, the Black Grotesque text mines sites of debasement as metaphoric debris with regenerative potential. The lower stratum of the body is the zone where degradation and renewal conjoin. Finest is thus also healed by the inappropriate intrusions of what lies beneath, in the lower bodily sphere, via acts of tactile and textual substitution. Finest Coon is virtually dead by the time he is rescued by Gus and Mabel. Mabel, who has likewise but lovingly killed her own father, makes every effort to save Finest, treating his burns with a balm made of cod liver oil, her own feces, and spit. She smears this salve on Finest's mouth, nose, and head and, by doing so meticulously and repeatedly, saves his life. In addition, the racially ambiguous, ginger-scented, beautiful prostitute aptly named Belle heals Finest's psychic wounds using her sex. As Finest discloses the details of his father's sexual abuse to Belle, she seeks his permission to caress his disfigured face, which she then kisses repeatedly:

> She kissed his chin. She kissed his mouth. His nose. The water filling up in his eyes. She kissed his cheeks and the lump on his head. The scars twitching and jumping on the side of his face and neck and when he tried to pull away . . . she shushed him and held him there and rocked him while he wept. . . . He stiffened against her and lifted her onto the lattice work, into one of the cutouts, and pushed her skirt back over her hips and the river rushed and the fire raged and she locked her legs around him and pulled him to her and they held each other as he wept and drove her into the lattice work and she kissed him and told him he was beautiful. He was beautiful.[48]

In a scene reminiscent of the Bakhtinian carnival, Belle and Finest spend the moonlit night drinking, smoking, and making love, as Finest weeps and Belle recognizes and repeatedly invokes his beauty. She handles Finest's scars, whose "twitching and jumping" evince the genitalization of black faces—the thoroughgoing sexualization, that is, of the dispossessed and disposable black. Finest's wounds that move are history's harms in animate flesh. His sex with Belle is thus a drama of overburdened engagement, where pulsating wounds are covered over and caressed. The lovers find pleasure in the risks of violation; their sex is described in one sentence, the length of a full paragraph, where the tension of driving and lifting and rushing and pushing and holding is built via the repetition of the simple conjunction *and*. In this fleeting moment of lovemaking, Finest's scars are transfigured from the materiality of unthinkable violation to the ecstatic and restorative signal of the orgasmic.

Even as I analyze such paradigmatically grotesque elements of Finest Coon's narrative, he is but one in a cast of main characters in a text overrun by scenes of despicable harm and compromised repair, some somberly and some satirically rendered. The familial genealogies that entwine and twist the color line in *Tradition* register a refusal of socially sanctioned, socially ordered relations. Belle is the biracial daughter of Beatrice Simler, a white woman who has had an affair with Gus and Mabel's father, the "Fix-it Man," who had worked in the Simler home.[49] Before it is revealed that Finest and Beatrice have the beautiful Belle in common, these two characters—the maimed black man and the mad white woman—are textual surrogates whose experiences mirror one another. Like Finest, Beatrice is the victim of child sexual abuse and incest; she gives birth to her father's child. Beatrice spends most of her adult life sleeping and drinking, wandering away from the family home, talking to herself, and trying to see the whole shape of things that catch her eyes. As a young man moving about the town, Finest is subject to public hysteria and derision, just as Beatrice's meandering and muttering frighten the town residents, for whom she is believed to be a "ghost and a witch."[50] As adults, both Beatrice and Finest retreat from language. And, when her husband dies, rather than leave his inheritance to their children, Beatrice wills the family fortune to Finest Coon.

Black Grotesquerie registers profound disbelief in the capacity of realist narrative to capture and convey the ineffable. *Tradition* withholds many of the root causes of its characters' actions as well as the satisfaction of their resolution. The main events of the novel simultaneously cut and elude. The characters seem driven less by desire than by appetites at once fragile and ravenous. Insofar as Black Grotesquerie intertwines corporeality and textuality, the novel replicates the form of its characters' unpredictable hunger. Sensual Belle dies twice. The first death is speculative, not physical. As the rumored third baby of Beatrice Simler, Belle is believed to have been smothered as an infant by her mother. The second murder is also at the hands of a family member, and this one takes. In the woods, Mabel shoots her half-sister twice, surprised to find the bullet "travel so fast through the air and rip through and take out a chunk of [Belle's] head."[51] Significantly, Mabel considers her hastening the death of her terminally ill father a mercy killing, and, despite her lifelong alcoholism, which follows Belle's death, she wonders if this murder were not the same.

Whether pronouncing a death that hasn't actually occurred (as in the case of Finest) or in producing the demise of a loved one (as in the case of her father), Mabel engages death, as does the novel, as an inevitable feature of black life, unchangeable except for its negotiable terms. In the bathing ritual that leads up to her giving her father a lethal overdose of pain medication and alcohol, Mabel carefully and lovingly washes the decrepit body of the Weesfree patriarch. She spreads a warm wet rag over his face, his eyes, his mouth, his neck, his collarbone, "his arms. His hands. His fingers. Underneath his nails. She washes his chest. Sunken and pockmarked. His belly and the rise in his hips. The nest of hair around his privates. The misshapen and shriveled privates themselves," his thighs, his back and buttocks, his feet.[52] The methodical procedure of the bath is reflected in Blackman's writing, a series of fragments that regard each body part as its own item in a tentative whole. The Black Grotesque entwinement of body and text is evident here. The love that undergirds the killing of what is already almost dead insinuates the unspeakable longings and unbearable remedies for black suffering to which Black Grotesquerie gives expression.

Black Grotesque scenes of traversal beyond and beneath the thresholds of life and death recur throughout *Tradition*. These traversals enact living on as a practice of preserving remnants, of making last what has already been ruined, as black modes of being. It is Finest Coon who discovers Belle's body in the woods. And, despite the shock of pain so unbearable that he loses temporarily the function of his legs, he grants her the balm of his touch and his words, as she had once offered him: "And when the feeling returned to his legs, he went to her and fell to his knees and held her there and rocked her, and after awhile he lay her back down and turned her on her side and he put his mouth to her ear and he whispered to her, to her soul. To calm it as she crossed."[53] As Belle leaves and Finest thereafter fades away, her death inaugurates the continuous process of living on for both characters. The precise reason for Mabel's killing of Belle as well as Finest's final words to her are conspicuously absent from the text. By withholding such significant details, the novel avoids teleological accounting for disastrous occurrences in the mode of realist narrative.

Tradition eschews the contained temporality of a single historical moment or central narrative event and instead portrays the ongoing terrors, injuries, and pleasures that typify the lives of those in subjugated collectivities. The novel's suspension of linearity reveals its skepticism about accretive racial progress. Taking place in stultified moments of existential doom and embodied demise, *Tradition* explores quotidian black life mired in broken, recursive time. The entwined narratives that make up the text linger in moments either anterior or posterior to markers of racial progress. For example, the novel portrays Obama as the hopeful senator campaigning to be the first African American president but not as the US president already in his second term, as was the case at the time of the novel's publication. In one of the 1930s chapters, Richard Wright is invoked not as a literary giant of the mid-twentieth century but as an author who has just finished an as-yet-unpublished novel with a protagonist named Bigger. Similarly, World War II is invoked through the return of shell-shocked soldiers, not through the recollection of heroic battles. The novel's cutting-and-roaming episodic structure is typical of Black Grotesquerie, as the grotesque engenders disharmonious, disintegrative shapes. Accordingly, the moment of arrival, of culmination in either definitive loss or achievement, is held in abeyance in *Tradition*, as the novel thematizes modes of black living on in the face of perpetual chaos and continued diminishment.

Black Grotesquerie conveys the failed discursive promise of black representation in historical, political, and institutional terms. It is a strategic mode of signification that relinquishes the politics of recognition, even as it registers the life-diminishing impacts of racism in the new century. An analysis of grotesquerie thereby shifts the discursive register of black political desire from the rhetoric of representation to one of endurance and from identity to intimacy. Black Grotesquerie thus answers Frank B. Wilderson III's call for a new "language of abstraction with explanatory powers emphatic enough to embrace the Black."[54] By combining literary and bodily form, Black Grotesquerie degrades literature from a position of symbolic and cultural elevation to a level of common sensuality and materiality, and it emerges consequently as an expressive mode uniquely capable of conveying *in textual form* what happens to shattered, subordinated subjects. Marked by structural ambiguity and excess, Black Grotesquerie undermines normative perception and action, renders contingent the presumed fixity of meaning, and ruptures the given world. As a practice and poetic of formal disintegration, Black Grotesquerie reminds us that contemporary practices of freedom must engage with loss (of traditions, movements, persons, political ideals), and, furthermore, that the sites and labors of loss might constitute, for African diasporic subjects, freedom's proper domain.

2

HOLLOWED BLACKNESS

For those beyond the periphery, beyond even a language of the margin, for those literally "outdoors" and therefore dead to others, there needs to be a theory profound enough to explain such a devastating existence.
—SHARON PATRICIA HOLLAND

Heed the hollow.
—MALCOLM TARIQ

HORIZONS

She writes:

> if we ever lose sight
> may there be a lamppost
> a moon, a star
> a guiding light
> house, some reservoir
> of echo and song within.

peel me into that little girl
again, into a dreamer
still developing her country
moving mountains
merging neighborhoods and cities
of skin and bone
fascinated by the sensational
happiness of low living lovers[1]

Aja Monet's poem "when in doubt" is a chronicle of what is yet to come and a prayer for the always already. It is addressed to little black girls or to the black girls that all black women once were, or to the black girl who resides still in the now grown-up black woman who speaks this poem, constitutes its shaper and reveler in prayer and poetic song. In the evocation of "we" is a verbal summons and instantiation of a collective of the lost. The poem gathers them up (those little girls of color lost to themselves, if not the wider world) and provides a directive, a direction. A geography of the internal emerges from the verse, a world accessible in corners and crevices, a place where the reverberations of speech and song smooth the rough ground of terrorized zones (whether failed homes, violent streets, or occupied lands). The poem intones these reverberations; it orients lost black girls inward—that is, to the private—toward interior dwellings, revealing the barely visible lights of their own world-making potential. "when in doubt" thereby consecrates the internal as a site of decolonial (de)territorialization, the fleshly ground of a girl child's dreaming, her own echo and bone the impenetrable borders of a sovereign place.

Born and raised in Brooklyn, New York, Aja Monet is a black woman poet, educator, performer, and activist of Cuban and Jamaican descent. She writes poems "textured with the sights and sounds of growing up in East New York in the nineties, attending school on the South Side of Chicago, then soaring all the way to the olive groves of Palestine." This description appears on the inside of the book jacket of her 2017 book of poetry, *My Mother Was a Freedom Fighter*. This description is thematic: it touches the surface of things, the landscapes of distressed worlds, and the kinds of sociality and feeling engendered by the particularities of place. "Peel me into that little girl," the speaker petitions,

still developing her country
moving mountains
merging neighborhoods
of skin and bone.[2]

Monet's poem focuses on black girls whom it directs to turn inward. For those readers not summoned by it, the poem provides an opportunity to enact reading practices of refusal—in other words, modes of aesthetic encounter that resist the will to interpretive capture and, furthermore, that reject the presumed transparency of black texts and knowability of black worlds. Conceptualizing black girl formation in terms of the intimate, the haptic, "when in doubt" ultimately empowers little black girls in the language of geopolitics—freed-up zones of habitation, mountains under their sway, bordered regions, cities within the folds of their hands. In so doing, the poem insinuates that it is within black girls, in their inhabitance of and relations *within* the interior—put forth in this chapter in the idiom of *Black Hollows*—that they may find horizons of livability.

In the previous chapter, I proffered Black Grotesquerie as an aesthetic modality concerned primarily with regenerative and recombinant techniques of African diasporic art- and world-making in the face of obliteration. In doing so, I made the case for a nonredemptive conception of black freedom that necessarily entails and reckons with irreversible displacement and loss. Contending with how racialized and gendered systems of captivity and control (from the plantation to the checkpoint to the prison) operate through the tyranny of compulsory visibility—that is, through techniques and technologies of ubiquitous surveillance, tracking, exhibit, and capture—the current chapter theorizes Black Hollows / Hollowed Blackness as an abolitionist aesthetic that reimagines and reconfigures the spatial terrains of black freedom. This aesthetic modality entwines liminal spatiality and raw emotion—or, more specifically, it navigates hideaway geographies and opaque enclosures to reveal the stifled affective range of bare life and the emotive drains of barely living.[3] As an artistic practice and as a hermeneutic for reading avant-gardist African diasporic expressive culture, Black Hollows may be understood as the hollowing out of representation via the sequestering of black subjectivities and the seclusion of black social formations. Textually and visually, Black Hollows depict (1) the material perimeters of caverns, ditches, basements, closets, attics that, at times, become sites of escape, momentary relief, or passage for black people fleeing racial and gendered horror; and (2) the emotional state of hollowness that indicates black shock, emptiness, fatigue, doneness. This chapter considers various forms of racialized capture and its attendant suffering to conceptualize Black Hollows, as the chapter dwells with black subjects who move into, sequester, enfold themselves, arise, burst forth from them. Figuring architectures of escape, racialized spatialization, and fugitive modalities of motion and habitation, I attend most assiduously to quiet black interiors.[4] In readings of the poetry of Aja Monet, Colson Whitehead's novel *The Underground Railroad*, and the visual art of Alexandria Smith, I show how persons gendered black and female survive and subsist in the rhetorics and the registers of what is hidden, what is hiding, what is low, and what is loving between hollowed out black subjects.

This chapters maps the artistic deployment of Black Hollows across three distinct expressive forms: the novel, visual art, and poetry. Building on Katherine McKittrick's theorization of the "garreted" enslaved person in flight, I first analyze the materialization of Black Hollows in Colson Whitehead's *The Underground Railroad*. In Whitehead's imaginative retelling, the Underground Railroad is not only a network of secret passageways and safe houses interwoven throughout the slave south that led fugitive slaves to northern freedom; it is also a literal, materialized railroad, accessed via trap doors, displaced floorboards, basements, and hidden caverns. Reading the novel's protagonist Cora in light of her literary forebear Linda Brent, I attend to the emancipatory strategies of going deep, of going under, of going within—for rest, for reflection, for restoration, and for respite. The chapter further develops my conceptualization of Black Hollows by theorizing specifically the importance of interstitial zones as sites of sanctuary and temporary reprieve for feminized black subjects. Completing my analysis of *The Underground Railroad*, I also explore the ways in which post-neo-slave narratives refuse diegetic transparency and determinate denouement. In so doing, they interrogate the very notion of racial progress for since slavery's formal abolition. The chapter concludes by studying the visual art by Alexandria Smith, whose primary figure of aesthetic visualization and multimedia production is a little black girl. Typically depicted in oversized fragments—a finger pointing, a braid sticking out, an arm reaching—the black girl body is mainly hidden, frequently rearranged, and bound within tight symmetrical spaces. In my reading of the enmeshed materialities of flesh and container in Smith's renderings of broken-up black girls, I ponder the necessity of recognition, rescue, and regard for subjects gendered black and female. I thereby illuminate specifically the Black Hollow that is forged within black girl intersubjectivity and intimacy. Attentive to the racialized and gendered violences that both cause and characterize the violability of black female subjects, this chapter conceives of Black Hollows specifically in performances of aesthetic, critical, and interpretive refusal (or rejection, obviation, forestallment, escape) in black avant-gardist texts that center black women and girls. Notably, by foregrounding the maneuvers of these most terrorized and aggrieved of black subjects, Black Hollows / Hollowed Blackness redirects the scholarly, legal, and political focus of black fugitivity from the outward and external outdoors to the internal and interior hollow.[5]

MOTILITY AND MATERIALITY IN THE UNDERGROUND

One of the poems in Malcolm's Tariq's award-winning collection *Heed the Hollow* is named for the debunked medical condition drapetomania. Etymologically, the pseudoscientific term conjoins two Greek terms, *drapetes,* which means "runaway," and particularly a runaway slave, and *mania,* which bespeaks frenzy or insanity. On one hand, the term characterizes the longing for freedom by the enslaved as a kind of derangement.[6] On the other, the term mobilizes the scientific and medicalized discourse of derangement to register the futility of any (and certainly of repeated) attempt(s) at escape. In the lines of Tariq's poem, the supposed derangement of fugitivity is transformed into dogged, relentless, magical daring.

<table>
<tr><td>forgive the swamp its magic</td><td>niggers</td></tr>
<tr><td>and mischief to grab onto them</td><td>who flee</td></tr>
<tr><td>in the crook of its mouth and</td><td>wait</td></tr>
<tr><td>one death for another</td><td>for whispers</td></tr>
<tr><td>to become rooted in miles of muck</td><td>to run</td></tr>
<tr><td>from the crocodile's teeth but never</td><td>back</td></tr>
<tr><td>to the crack of whips here</td><td>in waters</td></tr>
<tr><td>housing the thickness of death</td><td>and birth</td></tr>
<tr><td>entangled in ropes of smog</td><td>themselves</td></tr>
<tr><td>choosing to brave the swamp to bring</td><td>back</td></tr>
<tr><td>desire sick with the will to return</td><td>to life[7]</td></tr>
</table>

On the page, the poem appears to be comprised of two columns, each delineating or implying a separate poem and/or a separate speaker. A double-voiced and dialogic text, there is implied in its two columns a directive for reading and reciting. These columns embed and thus require a pause, a lingering on the last word of each line before reading the word in the next column or following the enjambment onto the next line. The poem is in this regard corporealized, textualizing the movement, looking scattered, and taking flight of the runaway through breaks and cuts in its lineation. The reader undertakes the steps and stops of the fugitive, the wandering and the wondering of where to go next, of those who have run and hidden themselves away.

The second chapter of Christina Sharpe's *In the Wake: On Blackness and Being,* entitled "The Hold," begins with two epigraphs. The second one—of particular concern here—is the Oxford English Dictionary definition of *hold*, which Sharpe reproduces in full: "A large space in the lower part of a ship or aircraft in which cargo is stowed. (of a ship or an aircraft); continue to follow (a particular course); keep or detain (someone); a fortress." Encapsulated in the simple definition of a word made legible via text and image throughout this chapter of Sharpe's study is an account of racialized terror and human bondage that began centuries ago in slave fortresses along the West African side of the Atlantic where captive Africans were warehoused. Trans/disfigured into (in)human cargo, they were held in slave ship hulls and transported across the ocean. For the black, the hold is a technology of commodity conversion; of psychic and corporeal disfigurement; of cultural unmaking; of sexual and gendered dispossession; of sustained, manufactured human misery; of debility, penality, and death. And, according to Sharpe, "the hold repeats and repeats and repeats in and into the present."[8] Life in the hold, which is all of black life in the United States, then and now, produces the interior Black Hollow.

My analysis of Colson Whitehead's *The Underground Railroad* opens with critical attention to the hold to elucidate the centrality of deathly captivity—in all of its architectural, conceptual, sociopolitical, metaphorical, and metaphysical manifestations—to the time-space of black existence in modernity. Sharpe's positioning of the hold of the slave ship as synecdochic site for the brutal unmaking of African diasporic subjects and cultures via the Middle Passage is instructive. The hold inaugurates the atrocities and agonies of racialized enslavement as well as its unceasing continuum of social, psychic, political, and economic reconfigurations.[9] In the current moment, the ruin of political disenfranchisement, of bodily and social curtailment, of resource and labor extraction, of gendered violence and sexualized harm, of the wearying out and wearing away of black lives initiated in the hold perdures. Sharpe underscores the architecture (i.e., the material confines of a watery underground prison) within a technology of oceanic transport to intimate the conditions of life for black subjects in the New World well into the catastrophic, new millennial present.

Colson Whitehead's *The Underground Railroad* is a fictionalized account of that historical—and fabled—network of black escape, fugitive affiliation, and communitarian ethics in the time of racial slavery. The primary conceit and fantastical element of the novel is its rendering of the Underground Railroad as a physical locomotive that travels interstate along a subterranean American landscape. In the novel the Underground Railroad not only evinces the hidden network of people and places linked in freedom pursuits on behalf of the enslaved; it also allegorizes unfreedom as the malignant underbelly of US sociocultural, economic, environmental, and jurispolitical formations. The novel follows its black fugitive slave-girl protagonist Cora from the Randall planation in Georgia on her northbound journey through various states. Rather than take Cora directly from slavery to freedom, the Underground Railroad transports her across state borders that iterate gruesome experiences of black subjugation, exploitation, and disposal that have taken place since slavery's formal abolition. Specifically, in different states along the route, Cora observes legal segregation and ritual lynching; the institutionalized abuse, experimentation, and theft of black bodies in pursuit of medical knowledges; the museumizing of racial slavery; and the spectacularization of black pain. In South Carolina, for example, while living in a boardinghouse room with other single African American women, she learns of the medical experimentation and forced sterilization to which the young women are unwittingly subject. In North Carolina, in an extreme and nightmarish iteration of legalized racial segregation, African Americans are prohibited from entering or residing in the state. As she rides through the town, traveling along a road obscenely called the Freedom Trail, Cora encounters miles-long rows of "corpses hung from trees as rotting ornaments" belonging to the formerly enslaved, freemen who refused to relinquish landed property, and other unfortunate black people with nowhere else to go.[10] The foundational disenfranchisement and gruesome maltreatment inflicted on African Americans are depicted as historical in the novel by virtue of its nineteenth-century setting. However, the rendering of the underground railroad as a mechanical locomotive that runs along an elaborate national railing system (which was not fully developed in all regions of the United States until the post-Reconstruction period) disarranges chronology. This underground railroad both literalizes political theories and communal enactments of black fugitivity in the antebellum era as well as reflects the intertwinement of legal segregation, industrial innovation, labor exploitation, and carceral capitalism of later periods.[11] The fantastical underground railroad of Whitehead's novel thus travels both geographically and temporally. The structural, legal, political and psychosocial negations of black life that are unveiled along its route counter notions of racial progress, as they continue into the (never-ending) catastrophic present—though, of course, in updated and altered forms of racialized abduction, instrumentalization, and collective ruin.

Thinking through Black Hollows as both resistive and aesthetic strategy necessitates an engagement with Katherine McKittrick's account of black women's geographies and their capacity to trouble sites of domination and social processes that negate black living. Because it subtends the spatial refuge, psychosocial ease, and affective relief of the hollow, I note here—that the racialized harm that Cora encounters throughout the lethal US landscape reflects in particular the dangers of publicness (i.e., collection, containment, exhibit, murder) of simply being present and capturable in open and external spaces for subjects gendered black and female. Building on Hortense Spillers's understanding of Harriet Jacobs's (pseudonymously Linda Brent's) escape from slavery via her disabling, if volitional, seven-year confinement in the garret of her grandmother's home as the fugitive practice of "garreting," Katherine McKittrick examines the ways in which black women resist captivity and commodification in the hold by burrowing further into its recesses, its concealed crevices, its hollows. She posits:

> That which is used to geographically displace and regulate black women during slavery, specifically patriarchal ways of seeing and white colonial desires for lands, free labor, and racial-sexual domination, rest on a tight hierarchy of racial power and knowledge that is spatially organized. This organization assumes white masculine knowledge and the logic of visualization, which both work to objectify Brent and her community and negate their unique sense of place. . . . Race, sex, and gender—her seeable body-scale—inscribe Brent as worthy of captivity, violence, punishment, and objectification; her bodily codes produce her slave master's surroundings. If the geographies of slavery are primarily about racial captivities and boundaries, and the garret is both a site of self-captivity and a loophole of retreat, it becomes increasingly clear that it is Brent's different sense of place that allows her to explore the possibilities in the existing landscape. The spaces Brent discloses, both in the landscape of slavery and through her sense of place, demonstrate an unresolved, but workable, opposition to geographic domination.[12]

McKittrick underscores the extent to which enslavement was itself a visual-spatial arrangement. By virtue of being seen—as the fungible commodity, property, and instrument of a gazing and enslaving white public—the black body was made vulnerable to apprehension, objectification, and sexualized and reproductive exploitation. With a panoramic view from her attic window of the slave community, Jacobs is able to expropriate the (patriarchal, scientific) power of the gaze: she witnesses the comings and goings of her tormentors as well the experiences of other enslaved black people. Her newfound authority as viewer and witness ultimately displaces white masculine knowledge, its presumed epistemic certainty, and its logics of visualization. Jacobs ultimately emerges as the foremost authority on the regime of racial slavery and the most compelling advocate for its abolition.

Jacobs's fugitive strategy is one of concealment within the domestic interiors of the slaveholding community. Rather than flee outright to the North and abandon her children and beloved kin, she chooses to confine herself in an attic—a garret, a tiny crawl and holding space—for seven years. During that time, Jacobs suffers innumerable mental and physical ailments and eventually becomes permanently disabled by virtue of her long confinement within a nominally free hollow. Nonetheless, as McKittrick notes, Jacobs's decision to remain within the hidden space of her grandmother's garret provides her with refuge and respite from the atrocities of human bondage. Reminiscent of Jacobs's seven-year confinement in her grandmother's garret, while waylaid in North Carolina the fugitive Cora is concealed for several months within the nook of the attic in the home of white abolitionists Martin and Ethel Wells. When she is awake and alert, Cora, like Jacobs, spends her days purveying the quotidian doings, comings, and goings of the townspeople, observing them from a jagged spyhole in the wall. During her nightly viewings Cora becomes an unwitting spectator to a weekly ritual of lynching African Americans to furnish the Freedom Trail with its rows of rotting corpses. Like Jacobs, Cora is debilitated by her time in the nook; she has little room to stretch her limbs in the cramped space, often suffers from a lack of adequate air, has to ration food and water, and suffers desperately for want of company. Like Jacobs, Cora has episodes of delirium and paralysis in which she loses consciousness and bodily movability. Principally, Cora takes after Jacobs in her preference for confinement within a tiny, enfeebling crawl space over the hazards of an outside landscape under white dominion.

It is important to emphasize here the gendered dimension of garreting. It is a strategy undertaken specifically by black subjects whose feminization within captivity makes them particularly vulnerable to being taken or had whenever they appear. Throughout Whitehead's *The Underground Railroad*, Black Hollows are sites that are either discovered or created within the deeper recesses of a domicile or a concealed zone within its vicinity, often leading to the stations and tunnels of the underground railroad. The sites of reprieve depicted in the novel are within the literal, material boxcars of the railroad and the caves, subterranean tunnels, basements, and crawl spaces that constitute its stops and hiding places. To resist the innumerable violations, impositions, uses, and injuries to which they are always susceptible, subjects gendered black and female develop an intimate awareness of crevices and corners as hideouts and temporary sites of sanctuary. It is the knowledge of the Black

Hollow that is sought by those who have been hollowed out that gives rise to black women's fugitive practices within private interiors, despite their liminality and temporariness.

In an exemplary scene in the novel, in order to escape Ridgeway, the unrelenting slave catcher who eventually abducts Cora from the Wellses' home in North Carolina, she garrets in a dank, filthy outhouse. The outhouse becomes in effect a Black Hollow:

> "I need to visit the outhouse," Cora said.
>
> The corners of his mouth sank. He gestured for her to walk in front. The steps to the back alley were slippery with vomit and he grabbed her elbow to steady her. Closing the outhouse door, shutting him out, was the purest pleasure she'd had in a long while.[13]

Though seemingly minor, this scene is noteworthy. Not only does Cora find momentary refuge in the small, unlit, and literally shitty wooden box but she also experiences a small reprieve from the slave catcher, who embodies militarism and murderous white supremacist (cis-hetero-)patriarchy. It is Ridgeway who pronounces to Cora (and, by extension, the reader) the ethos and underlying ideology of US national formation. He describes "the American spirit, the one that called us from the Old world to the New, to conquer and build and civilize. And to destroy what needs to be destroyed. To lift up the lesser races. If not lift up, subjugate. And if not subjugate, exterminate. Our destiny by divine prescription—the American imperative."[14] As the primary slavecatcher in the novel, Ridgeway is also the primary antagonist; his main narrative purpose is to dismantle the fugitive endeavor. As each attempted or successful slave escape fundamentally undermines the logics and disorders the arrangements of racial slavery, Ridgeway acts as the legitimate, legalistic mechanism of racist reordering. A forerunner to the police—other characters refer to him as "the heat"—Ridgeway employs predatory techniques of surveillance, pursuit, and entrapment to return fugitives to their former owners.[15] Despite his general omnipresence, during Cora's brief seclusion in the hollow of the outhouse Ridgeway is transformed into nothing more than "a man talking to an outhouse door, waiting for someone to wipe her ass." And Cora, hidden for just this instant in a dark, dirty outhouse, overhears music from next door and contemplates the enthralling tactility of slow dancing and wonders about the fate and freedom of black people.[16] Overall, Whitehead's fictional account of the Underground Railroad materializes Black Hollows as spatial-relational architectures of fleeting safety, temporary respite, and (always only) evanescent liberation for racialized, gendered subjects.

AN INTERSTITIAL ZONE

To be hollowed out is to be bereft of feeling and lost to meaning. To be hollowed out is to be at risk of bottoming out. The index of bodily hollows is the exhaustion of sociopolitical and civic annihilation that punctuates the inhalation and exhalation of live blackened bodies. It can register as the lost concern for the rhythms of one's own breath and the entirety of social life. Hollowness is embodied in the fallen shoulders, the pounding head, the upturned belly, the empty chest of black subjects who are by now tired of being tired. As embodied affect, hollowness does not regard or obey the commands or flows of progressive temporalities. The expedited corporeal overthrow of shock produces immediate hollowness, and the worn-down, debilitated body is too slow to adhere to the pressures of normative or narrative time. To be hollowed out is to land at the threshold of death, which either culminates in demise or facilitates a crossing onto the precipice of rebirth, toward the promise of being filled anew.

By the time she makes her escape, Mabel, Cora's mother, is hollowed out. Readers don't learn of Mabel's fate until the end of *The Underground Railroad*, in the brief penultimate chapter in which her solitary, if serene, death in a swamp not far from the Randall plantation (from which she fled the previous day) is described. Throughout the text Mabel has a mythological, haunting presence: as the only slave from the Randall plantation to run and stay away, evading recapture even by the expert and invariably effective slave catcher Ridgeway, and as the enslaved black mother who defies the psychic and affective bonds of maternity (a logic of naturalized confinement on which slaveowners relied to keep feminized labor in bondage and in place) to leave behind her only child in permanent, miserable enslavement. Aside from the primal desire of the enslaved to be free, Mabel's motivation for escaping is undisclosed until that eponymous chapter: How did she manage after all to leave her little girl alone, abject, and entirely susceptible to the totalized dispossession, the gendered depredations, the mundane miseries, the full and brutal instrumentalization by others that racial slavery legislated and literalized? As the text fundamentally withholds Mabel (as a character whose actions, thoughts, and intentions are narrativized), she moves throughout the novel as a ghost. Even prior to the revelation of her death, she is glimpsed by other characters—and thus by readers—through brief, imperfect memories, traces of dialogue, scenes that depict her action and speculate about her intention. Vanished and haunting as a result, Mabel serves as both an aspiration and a guide to other captives on the Randall plantation, a virtual North Star to those who would abscond from that domain of white power, profit, and pleasure. Mabel's disappearance potentiates Cora, who, despite early abandonment and orphanhood, undertakes the fugitive's mission aboard the materialized, locomotive underground railroad.

Mabel's flight from the Randall plantation seemingly epitomizes the core deficiencies that have been attributed to black motherhood: ineptitude or inadequacy in the capacity and delivery of suitable nurturance, attachment, protection, and care for progeny.[17] Under the regime of slavery black maternity was stripped of all legal protection and of any normative cultural regard and reduced to the financialization of rape for the mass (re)production of enslaved human capital. For the enslaved, that is, motherhood was excluded from the norms of social meaning, domestic enclosure and stabilization, and (phantasmagorical) patriarchal prolificacy and national prosperity. It is precisely this neutralization of black mothering under the regime of generational enslavement that drives Mabel's despondency and her desperate escape. Her decision to flee is instantaneous, borne of a midnight moment of contemplation of three separate incidents emblematic of the hurts and hazards of black mothering in bondage: the death of Mabel's beloved man, Grayson the Sweet, who had promised and genuinely planned to purchase their freedom but who died of fever without learning she was pregnant with Cora; the suicide of the young slave Polly after the stillborn delivery of her baby girl; and Mabel's own rape and forced concubinage by the young black overseer Moses. Recalling how painstakingly Mose's mother fought to preserve his life during a season of black infant deaths on the Randall Plantation, Mabel thinks: "Men [start] off good and then the world makes them mean. The world is mean from the start and gets meaner every day. It uses you up until you only dream of death."[18] Collectively, these three black maternal occurrences define for Mabel not only the "meanness" of men, the distorted and embittering social universe inhabited by human others on the slave plantation but also the meanness of the world itself—in which white entitlement and white dominion over black women's corporeality, sexuality, and reproductivity are paradoxically so embedded and so unbound that they feel like an abominable and heartbreaking cosmological design aimed at the wholesale degradation and ruin of the black. Mabel resolves to run.

A few miles from the Randall plantation, in the swamp—that interstitial zone comprised of and in between earth and water—Mabel goes down. Twice. Within histories, literatures, and political theories of black fugitivity, the swamp delineates the border (spatial, psychic, material, environmental) between enslavement and emancipation.[19] In my analysis, the swamp distinguishes the Black Hollow as a site of (only ever liminal and momentary) black freedom from the general open terrain of the outside—with its ever-present risks of exposure, abduction, exploitation, and gruesome demise for the black subject. In her comprehensive history of the Underground Railroad, *Free Black Communities and the Underground Railroad*, Cheryl Janifer LaRoche discusses the importance of "inaccessible land" and concealed spaces in the fugitive's bid for freedom. She argues that

> the landscape is an intimate yet underexplored component of the Black experience, where danger lurked and freedom beaconed. Although the land was a site of disorientation, hardship, frostbite, and starvation, it also held crucial pathways out of slavery. Generations of escapees on the Underground Railroad turned to the sheltering anonymity of the land to conceal their journey. . . .
>
> Those who managed successful escapes and those who aided them needed to overcome physical and psychological boundaries. Broadly defined in cultural landscape terms, the Underground Railroad encompassed not only houses but each route forged by the enslaved, each track to freedom enmeshed in what the National Park Service identifies as a "vast network of paths and roads, through swamps and over mountains, along and across rivers and even by sea." Tree hollows, caves, precipices, and sinkholes, high ground and lookout points, forests, thickets, and southern swamps formed natural barriers that protected freedom seekers from their would-be captors. The use of inaccessible land, such as the Great Dismal Swamp, was a hallmark of escape, ensuring success and making the creation of new communities possible.[20]

Ontologically, topographically, and operationally, the slave plantation was a domestic and agricultural prison for the expropriation of labor, proprietary consolidation, routine torture, obscene amusements, and monetary accumulation. Hemmed in at times by vast inhospitable lands, enslaved captives who fled often encountered and navigated unknown and sometimes treacherous landscapes. The swamp thus operates as a crucial site of traversal and transfiguration for the terrified and weary enslaved who would prefer the untold dangers of the swamp (with its limited pathways and numerous lethal species) to the quotidian horrors of each day in slavery.

As an indomitable and inaccessible terrain of enmeshed water and land, and as a rich ecosystem of sustained and secluded life forms, the swamp is central to cartographies of black fugitivity and to imaginaries of black freedom. To adumbrate those imaginaries, I linger here with the distinctions between the two incidents in which Mabel is swallowed by the swamp, the first when she first tastes freedom and the second when she fatally succumbs:

> Mabel tripped over a cypress root and went sprawling into the water. She staggered through the reeds to the island ahead and flattened on the ground. Didn't know how long she had been running. Panting and tuckered out.
>
> She took a turnip from her sack. It was young and tender-soft, and she took a bite. The sweetest crop she'd ever raised in Ajarry's plot, even with the taste of the marsh water. Her mother had left that in her inheritance, at least, a tidy plot to watch over. You're supposed to pass on something useful to your children. . . .
>
> She lay on her back and ate another turnip. Without the sound of her splashing and huffing, the noises of the swamp resumed. The spadefoot toads and turtles and slithering creatures, the chattering of black insects. Above—through the leaves and branches of the black-water trees—the scrolled before her, new constellations wheeling in the darkness as she relaxed. No patrollers, no bosses, no cries of anguish to induct her into another's despair. No cabin walls shuttling her through the night seas like the hold of slave ship. Sandhill cranes and warblers, otters splashing. On the bed of damp earth, her breathing slowed and that which separated her from the swamp disappeared. She was free.
>
> This moment.[21]

Enslaved captives spent their lives tethered in place in a static, permanent state of unfreedom, unrecognized as civically entitled entities before the law and without recourse to an administrative or governance authority that might intervene on their behalf. Socially, politically, and civilly dead, the enslaved were, in effect, exiled from the domain of the living.[22] It is significant, then, that Mabel's first fall unites her with the aliveness of the swamp. A runaway from the Randall plantation, Mabel arrives at this place physically worn and emotionally hollowed—staggering, flattened, panting and tuckered out. Eschewing anthropocentric priority, she joins with the various creatures whose habitat she has entered and with whom she shares this rare moment of rest. Listening to the nighttime sounds of the swamp—a cacophony of insects, amphibians, and reptiles—Mabel relaxes into the wet earth that has broken her fall, and she eats the products of her mother's garden. Manifestations of a maternal inheritance that contests and remediates the enslaved's predicament of natal alienation, the soft, sweet turnips nourish and replenish her.[23] Momentarily restored by her retreat into watery earth, in the Black Hollow of the swamp, Mabel conceptualizes black freedom—an interstitial zone, an obscure tiny place, a pause in the inhuman rhythms and routines of plantation modernity, a hollow.[24]

> She had to go back. The girl [Cora] was waiting on her. This would have to do for now.... She would keep this moment close, her own treasure. When she found the words to share it with Cora, the girl would understand there was something beyond the plantation, past all she knew....
>
> The snake found her not long into her return. She was wending through a cluster of stiff reeds when she disturbed its rest. The cottonmouth bit her twice, in the calf and deep in the meat of her thigh. No sound but pain. Mabel refused to believe it. It was a water snake, it had to be. Ornery but harmless. When her mouth went minty and her leg tingled, she knew. She made it another mile. She had dropped her sack along the way, lost her course in the black water. She could have made it farther—working Randall land had made her strong, strong in body if nothing else—but she stumbled onto a bed of soft moss and it felt right. She said, Here, and the swamp swallowed her up.[25]

As I theorize Black Hollows—particularly in terms to those gendered black and female—it is important to highlight the extractive labor formations that undergird the relational dynamics between these subjects and others. As her motivation for fleeing the Randall plantation is intimately tied to black maternity under conditions of enslaved captivity, Mabel seeks and takes refuge from the anguish of mothering an enslaved black girl—the agonies of loss, of irrelevance, of helplessness, of theft. The Black Hollow is defined in part by the inherent brevity of any reprieve granted (or taken by) hollowed-out black subjects. As she comes to understand black freedom as brief and bare, as evanescent and interstitial, Mabel realizes that this new knowledge constitutes a shareable inheritance between the enslaved mother and progeny. Black freedom is like the tiny plot of garden bequeathed by *her* mother that furnished the turnips. Compelled to her daughter by this realization, Mabel dies not far from the Randall plantation in the act of return.

Even as the swamp configures momentary sanctuary for the fugitive from racial slavery, it nonetheless reveals the inherent dangerousness of the outdoors—of just being outside—for black subjects in general by underscoring the fundamental susceptibility of black people to extreme suffering and untimely death. Put plainly, Mabel's eventual death in the swamp underscores the basic treachery of any landscape under white supremacist rule. As within the slave plantation, the natural environs surrounding architectures of human bondage were patrolled by those charged with maintaining it: slave catchers and patrollers, marauding white mobs, flesh-eating hunting dogs, and so on.[26] Accordingly, in Whitehead's *The Underground Railroad* the successful navigation of the swamp prefigures successful escape from slavery.

This sustained, substrative unknowability—diegetic, dialogic, structural, climactic—qualifies *The Underground Railroad* as a post-neo-slave narrative. Margo Crawford, who has coined the term and theorized its generic components, describes the "architecture of the post-neo-slave narrative [as] the unknowable and the uncontainable."[27] In her analysis of Colson Whitehead's *The Underground Railroad*, Gabriella Friedman argues that "Blackness is opaque, not transparent; Black interiority is not available to the reader of Whitehead's novel."[28] Due to the perpetually deferred promise of delivery to a free state (or state of freedom), Cora's repeated escapes onto the locomotive underground railroad deliver her to unknown territories and unanticipated terrains: "the barn of shackles, the hole in the earth, this broken-down boxcar—the heading of the underground railroad was laid in the direction of the bizarre."[29] Margo Crawford's theorization of the post-neo-slave narrative in contradistinction to the neo-slave narrative is instructive here: even though both black literary genres are late twentieth-century, fictionalized accounts of New World slavery, neo–slave narratives aim for historic and experiential precision in their renderings of racial slavery.[30] Recognizing nineteenth-century limitations on and circumscriptions of public and publishable speech, neo–slave narratives imaginatively language psychic interiors, experiences, and aspirations of the enslaved by supplementing the silences, innuendos, fissures in narratives of slavery authored in the nineteenth century. Rising to prominence in the United States in the period immediately following the civil rights movement, neo–slave narratives incorporate and expand the generic components of antebellum slave narratives in an attempt to make slavery familiar—intimate, even—to contemporary audiences. In so doing, neo–slave narratives deploy rhetorical and narratological features to forge a sentimental and sympathetic identification with the reader.[31] This sympathetic identification augments, within the realm of cultural production, the collective political plea of African Americans for the unqualified resources and protections of citizenship during and after the civil rights movement.

Post-neo-slave narratives, by comparison, do not evidence such clear political intent. A fugitive form of new millennial black literary output, they obfuscate, conceal, disassemble, and turn away from the audience. Impeding any sympathetic identification or interpretive presumption on the part of contemporary readers, post-neo-slave narratives maintain first and foremost the illegibility and multiplicity of slavery's horrors. Crawford contends:

> If the neo-slave narrative is revisionist history, the post-neo-slave narrative is a move from the literary imagination that fills in the gaps (what historians cannot know) to the refusal to fill in the gaps but to linger in the unknown. If the neo-slave narrative builds on the form of nineteenth-century slave narratives, the post-neo-slave narrative may be the narratives that stop building on and begin to improvise more fully.[32]

The defining distinction between neo–slave narratives and post-neo-slave narratives is the latter's refusal to accede to the representation, in language, of slavery's deep, defining wretchedness or its representability in literary form. By way of experimental modes of storytelling, post-neo-slave narratives demonstrate the extent to which racial slavery defies historicity, generic constraint, epistemic certainty, and readerly comprehension. Furthermore, post-neo-slave narrative unsettle political pleas and proscriptive paradigms for black racial uplift in *any* era, implying ultimately that—as is the case for Cora—freedom is neither an achievable nor preservable state for the enslaved captives of the New World or for their descendants.

The conclusion of *The Underground Railroad* makes this point startingly clear, as the all-black settlement where Cora finally finds a safe and apparently sustainable home—and that in many ways bespeaks black political arrival, civic accomplishment, and socioeconomic security—is ultimately destroyed from without as within. After escaping from the slave catcher Ridgeway with the help of armed black men, Cora takes her penultimate journey aboard the underground railroad. It delivers her, alongside her two rescuers, Royal and Red, to the Valentine farm, an all-black, free community in Indiana. Established by John Valentine, a free and phenotypically white African American along with his wife, Gloria, the Valentine farm is an independent and prosperous black community within an unsettled and still developing state.[33] Temporally unbound, the Valentine farm iterates diasporic maroon societies that developed throughout the Atlantic world in the era of modern racial slavery; the all-black freedmen's towns that emerged across the United States during the post-Reconstruction era; and abolitionist, decolonial idylls of imagined, free black futures. That some of the members of the Valentine farm bear arms not only reflects willful, communal self-defense but also reveals black militarism as a viable strategy of liberative endeavor, socioeconomic and civic establishment, communal protest, and collective protection on behalf of black lives. Possessed of its own school, an educational and culturally affirming library, vast acreages for agricultural production, and numerous cottages for its growing black population, the Valentine farm is a haven for fugitive and free black people alike.

Across the treacherous domains of fugitive endeavor, escape, and existence that are depicted throughout Whitehead's novel, the Valentine farm stands as the emblem of arrival, of landing. This is underscored by two significant moments in the text: one in which Cora allows herself intimacy with Royal, with whom she is falling in love, and the other in which the pair descend into one of the underground railroad's tunnels not far from Valentine farm. Situated beneath an abandoned and long-uninhabited cottage, this station marks the seeming end of the underground railroad. Vivified even in its discard, the decrepit old cottage offers a route to freedom that it resolutely conceals. Cora follows Royal as he reveals two trapdoors, and the two descend the staircases following each:

> It was the sorriest, saddest station yet. There was no drop to the tracks—the rails started at the end of the steps and jetted into the dark tunnel. A small handcar rested on the tracks, its iron pump waiting for a human hand to animate it. As in the mica mine in North Carolina, long wooden planks and struts buttressed the walls and ceiling. . . .
>
> A notion crept over her like a shadow: that this was not the start of the line but its terminus. Construction hadn't started beneath the house but at the other end of the black hole. As if in the world there were no places to escape to, only places to flee.[34]

After contemplating her arrival at Valentine and reminiscing about the story of its establishment—John Valentine's determination to assist every fugitive slave in need of sustenance and sanctuary—Cora resolves to stay on the farm. With its promises of black self-possession and social belonging, the community feels to her like the final destination of the underground railroad, a cumulative and fitting terminus for all of the exhausted labor that has characterized both her bondage and escape. It is after this moment in the desolate underground station that Cora allows herself to share physical intimacy with Royal—a corporeal and sensual arrival (or landing) of sorts, given that a brutal gang rape in her girlhood has previously prevented Cora from participating in intimate or romantic touch.

The specific details of Cora's one night with Royal are notably absent from the text, referenced only in innuendo and, later, in a dream. By withholding such significant details, the novel avoids the sexualized consumption of racialized, gendered characters by the audience. In a significant departure from the modes and objectives of realist narratives that portray black life-worlds, the novel retains the secrecy, the privacy, of black interiors. The novel is similarly reticent about the cause of the destruction of the Valentine farm and the murder of so many of its inhabitants, which occurs soon after the revelation of the final stop of the underground railroad. Whether as a result of differing political philosophies among members of the community regarding its proper future—that is, the pace and praxes of racial uplift—or as a consequence of growing white resentment of the all-black town in Indiana, or the machinations of the slave catcher Ridgeway (who once again kidnaps Cora), the novel withholds the cause of and invites speculation about the ambush on the Valentine farm. In so doing, the text eschews progressive teleology and disallows diegetic transparency.

Throughout *The Underground Railroad*, Whitehead engages in the literary practice of black abstraction and the textual deployment of Black Hollows. The novel concludes with a final return to the desolate, subterranean station near Valentine farm. Driven there by Ridgeway at gunpoint, Cora manages to wrest her body free of the slave catcher and grabs the iron pump of the lone handcar:

> She pumped and pumped and rolled out of the light. Into the tunnel that no one had made, that led nowhere.
>
> She discovered a rhythm pumping her arms, throwing herself into movement. Into northness. Was she traveling through the tunnel or digging it? Each time she brought her arms down on the lever, she drove a pickax into the rock, swung a ledge onto a railroad spike....
>
> She put miles behind her, put behind her the counterfeit sanctuaries and endless chains, the murder of Valentine farm. There was only the darkness of the tunnel, and somewhere ahead, an exit. Or a dead end, if that is what fate decreed—nothing but a blank, pitiless wall. The last bitter joke. Finally spent, she curled on the handcar and dozed, aloft in the darkness as if nestled in the deepest recess of the night sky.[35]

Always a fugitive affair, evanescent and evolving, black freedom is neither a fixed state nor a definitive site of arrival. The pursuit of freedom—no matter how perilous, or arduous, or continuous—is all that brings the black into proximate relation with it. Cora's nestled rest in the handcar is reminiscent of Mabel's sojourn in the swamp. As throughout the novel Cora makes repeated attempts to escape capture, the novel textualizes the evasion of capture vis-à-vis the reader. Concealed by the paltry frame of a moving wooden box atop a track inside a tunnel forged by the labor of her own arms, Cora heads off the page in the direction of the unknown and the undisclosed.

RESCUE, REGARD, RESONANCE

To be disappeared is a harrowing experience. To feel oneself as distinctly and wholly made—as shaped by the accretion of discrete lived moments, as the unique summary of aversions and preferences, and as reflected in a particular disposition or affective universe—and to then fail to register or resonate in the domain of human relations is a violent undoing. The essential harms of containment, of bodily expropriation, of curtailed movement, of inadequate sustenance, of debilitated and weary living; the violences, in other words, that define living in the afterlives of slavery's proscriptive social death haunt every relational instance in which a black person finds herself invalidated and invisiblized. I open this final section, which reads the visual art of Alexandria Smith, with the admission of the potential dangers of concealment (of being hidden or stowed away at all) for racialized, gendered, sexualized subjects who do not figure in the social domain and who fail to matter as worthwhile and protectable life forms in psychic and jurispolitical ones. While my conceptualization of Black Hollows advances a fugitive black aesthetic and sociopolitical strategy that is oriented toward obscurity, privacy, and reprieve, it nonetheless takes seriously the need for recognition, for community, and for witness of the vulnerable and the abandoned. Black Hollows / Hollowed Blackness is an abolitionist aesthetic, not an isolationist one. In conversation with central black feminist tenets of love and relation, I study visual art by Alexandria Smith, an accomplished African American multimedia visual artist and co-organizer of the collective Black Women Artists for Black Lives Matter, to argue that the rallying cry of the global movement for Black lives—that is, that Black Lives Matter—is (or must be) both an outward and intramural address. Demonstrating how the undisclosed and unmapped interiors of the Black Hollow give rise to innovative praxes of regard, rescue, and resonance for subjects gendered black and female, this section further attends to the aesthetic conjuration and bodily communion of those who are always at risk of being thrown away and hollowed out.

Kevin Quashie theorizes the interior as an essential site of black becoming, of liberative, living experimentation—what he calls "a space of wild selffullness." Though not entirely independent of or antagonistic to the reach of conquest, the ravages of human captivity and political terror, or the unrelenting trauma of gendered and sexualized dispossession, the interior nonetheless delineates a barrier to all of these, designating an unchartered secret place on the inside and a wild-style ecosystem of black subjectification. The interior, as Quashie describes it,

> is the inner reservoir of thoughts, feelings, desires, fears, ambitions that shape a human self.... The interior is expansive, voluptuous, creative; impulsive and dangerous... akin to hunger, memory, forgetting, the edges of all the humanness one has.... The interior shifts in regard to life's stimuli but it is neither resistant to nor overdetermined by the vagaries of the outer world. The interior has its own ineffable integrity and it is a stay against the social world.[36]

Though responsive to what happens beyond it, the internal offers a site of protection and respite. Given its ineffable integrity and its fundamentally inarticulable quality, to give language to black interior life requires the deformation of available expressive forms. In other words, the stylized production of black psychic and social interiors gives rise to nuanced aesthetic, relational, ethical, and sociopolitical experimentation in a modality conceptualized throughout this chapter as Black Hollows / Hollowed Blackness.

Reflecting on the multimedia images that comprise her first solo exhibit at Boston University's Stone Gallery in November 2018, entitled *A Litany for Survival*, Alexandria Smith queries, "How can these figures both be present and invisible at the same time? How can these figures both be independent but also together, and sort of joined, and be a part of their environment literally?"[37] Smith interrogates and pursues an artistic practice that produces black presence without a(n) (inevitable, presumed necessary) correlative publicness. In other words, she demonstrates blackness *is* "here" without necessarily putting it "out there"—for theft, for commodification, for judgment, for discard. Whether presented in collage or as cartoons, the principal figures in Smith's work are little black girls. Typically depicted in oversized fragments—a finger pointing, a braid sticking out, an arm reaching—the black girl body in Smith's work is mainly hidden, frequently rearranged, and bound within tight symmetrical spaces. The cartoonish little black girl of Smith's figuration hides or is crammed into corners and closets, half-hides or is submerged in water. Pigtails, eyes, hands, and legs stretch into characters and landscapes, constituting types of black girls and typographies of black girl subjectivities. Like the garreted enslaved girl in Harriet Jacobs's *Incidents*, Smith's little black girls peek and poke and point. Depicted as solitary figures, these black girls who blend into backgrounds appear to seek recognition or await rescue. The enmeshed materialities of flesh and container in

Smith's renderings of broken-up black girls rework the relation of fright and relief through the mechanism of anticipated looking. In other words, underlying Smith's fragmented, isolated, hollowed-out black girls is a comment on the general need of black female and femme subjects for someone's protective interest and rescue—or, in other words, their need for regard.

In her essay "To Be Announced: Radical Praxis or Knowing (at) the Limits of Justice," Denise Ferreira da Silva proffers a meditation on the meaning and measure of blackness that grapples with its value and excess, or its value in excess. Noting the life-snuffing harms that attend and abbreviate black living, da Silva reads the female black as the figure that epitomizes racialized violence even as such violence gets obscured by her gendered specificity. In other words, the subject who is gendered black and female bears the primary *and* the most brutal incarnations of interpersonal, social, and structural commodification and subordination that are characteristic of racist regimes. Da Silva considers the efficacy and the interventional capacity of knowledge production to remediate the commodification, subordination, extermination of black people. She notes that "any apparatus deployed in the knowledge of human affairs produce the very affairs they acquire."[38] The mimetic representation of harm relies upon that harm and reproduces it. Da Silva turns to "the radical potential the juridicoeconomic figure of the (native/enslaved) female—namely, her sexual body, which insists on signifying Other-wise, [that] troubles representation."[39] She argues convincingly that the racialized and gendered excesses of the female black account for her failure to appear or to signify—to be captured, as it were.

Alexandria Smith's 2018 exhibit "A Litany for Survival" depicts racialized, feminized figures in interiorized dwellings, in private communion. The individual artworks that comprise the installation pursue simultaneously an investigation of Du Boisian double-consciousness in black women's subjective development and a celebration of the relational practices of black feminine and black feminist communality. Amid hideouts, watery enclaves, and fragmented terrain, Smith's figural abstractions mirror, double, and shadow one another. Arches signify doorways and movement; mirrors signify looking and the promise of being beheld; water signifies modes of passage and potentiated renewal. Oversized and bound together in reflexive poses, Smith's racialized, gendered figures angle toward each other and subtly touch. Against blue and black and brown and purple canvases, the female blacks of Smith's surreal, cartoonish world are never isolated or alone as in her earlier works. In fact, their togetherness seems to be the point. Rendered abstractly in confrontational colors and muted undertones, Smith's multimedia images are untimely.

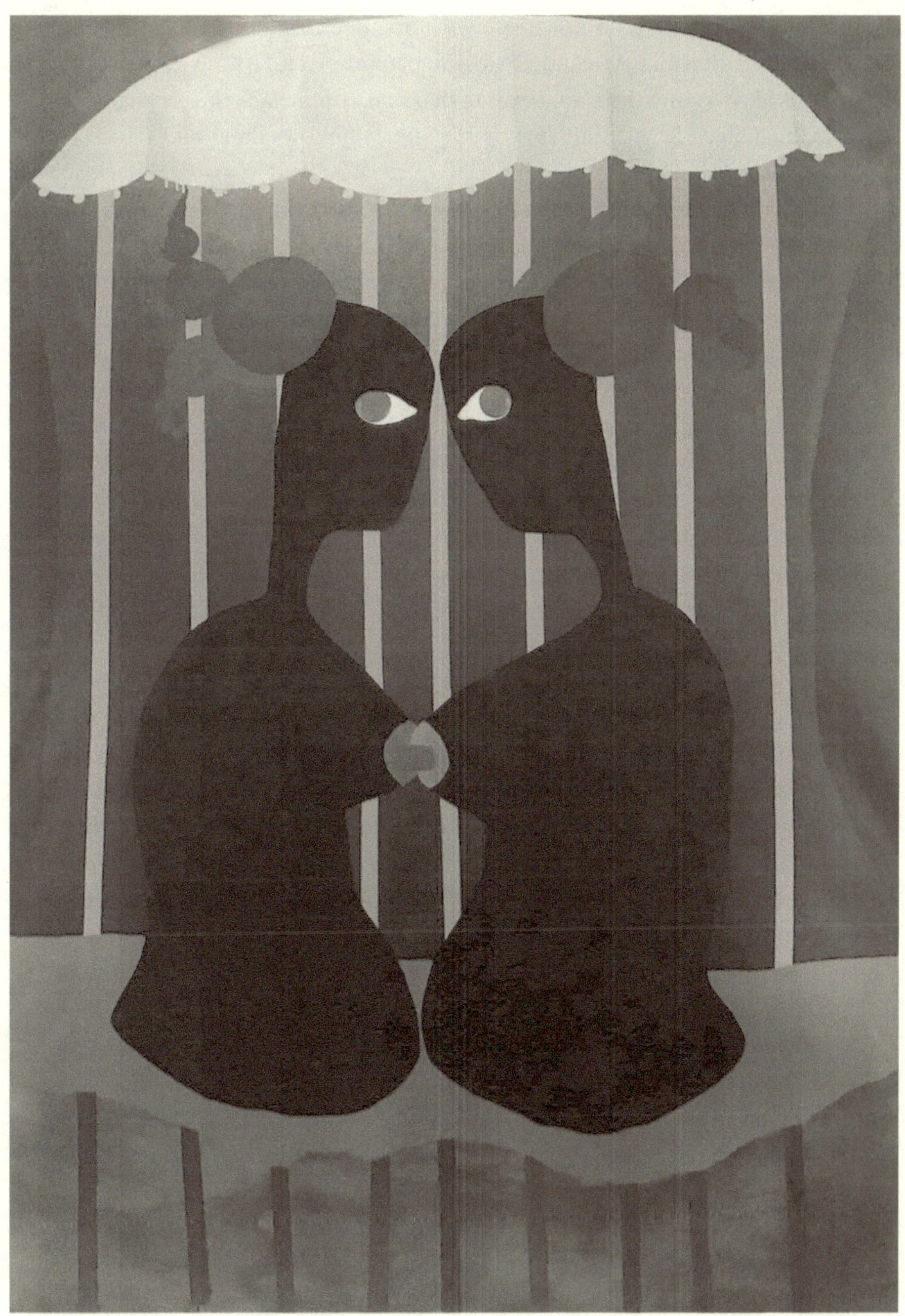

FIGURE 2.1 Alexandria Smith, *The Skin We Speak*, 2018. Ink, collage, plant materials, and plastic pearls on Mylar, 53 × 87 in. Courtesy of the artist and Lachell Workman Photography.

In other words, they do not display events, occurrences, happenings but, rather, their aftermaths (whether violent, playful, erotic) within home-spaces. Instead of revealing the signal events that constitute black life (or that shape individual black lives), Smith's artistic practice hollows them out.

An example: Alexandria Smith's *The Skin We Speak* visualizes black survival as a black feminine pairing. Staging the mirroring that insinuates selfhood (or exterior completeness and interior coherence), the painting depicts two blackened, seemingly female figures under an umbrella, canopy, or other protective cover. Held within the other's permanent gaze and yet with one eye visibly askance, the figures look *at* each other while simultaneously looking *out* for one another. The water that rises to the waists of both figures is suggestive of transatlantic crossings or displacements, and their mirroring is suggestive of having been found. Visualizing Black Hollows / Hollowed Blackness, the figures refuse a certain kind of audience engagement or interpretive authority; in fact, their intimacy nearly shames the viewer as an unwelcome, voyeuristic onlooker. The intimate touch of the figures registers an embrace. This embrace is not, however, a grasping or folding into of arms, which in their notable absence insinuates the expropriation of the body's labor—the dispossession of arms and hands. Instead, these figures touch at the breasts—the site of femininized beauty and other-nurturance. Missing arms and with breasts hanging low, the figures bespeak both expropriated gendered labor and the erotic potential of (con)joining. Their doubling gestures simultaneously to an intersubjective and a social practice that holds black women individually and collectively in each other's place. In *The Skin We Speak*, the emergence of the black female subject depends upon a togetherness that recognizes and rescues the self as the multiplicitous, abandoned, hollowed-out other—and that speaks in hushed tones of browns and oranges and blacks and blues.

bell hooks argues that love is the key to radical black politics. She describes love "as the practice of freedom" and reminds us that "when choosing love we also choose to live in community."[40] Alexandria Smith's piece *The Incognegroes* dramatizes community—in glorious choreographed black female movement. Modeled after Marcel Duchamp's modernist classic *Nude Descending a Staircase, No. 2*, Smith's piece depicts four female figures in graded shades of blues, blacks, and grays. The gradient color palette differentiates the figures—perhaps by region, by class, by epoch, by complexion. *Incognegro* most famously refers to racially ambiguous black subjects or those who do not signify blackness in publicly legible ways. One large eye conveys the work of looking, whether in a mirror or at the world, and thus of consciousness on

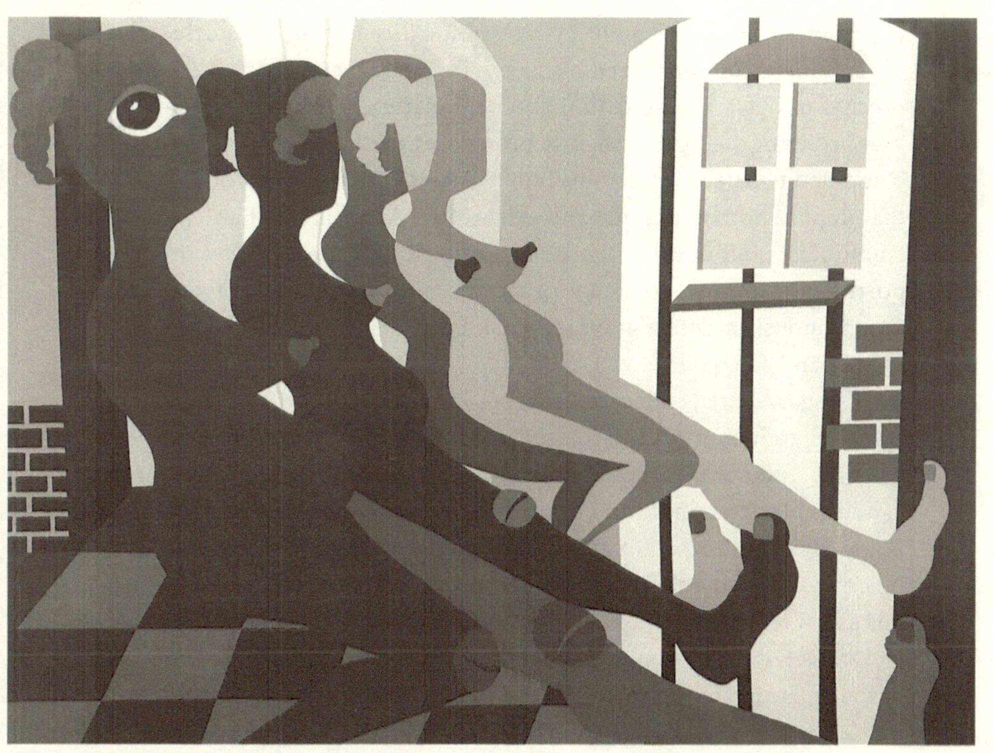

FIGURE 2.2 Alexandria Smith, *The Incognegroes*, 2018. Acrylic, oil, and enamel on canvas, 60 × 72 in. Courtesy of the artist and Lachell Workman Photography.

behalf of the collective. With silhouetted doubles or shadows on either side of a domesticized interior, the image alerts viewers to geometric lines, shapes, and textures of a domicile, while the background geometry of brick and steel conveys urban dwelling. The painting visualizes black women becoming themselves in the good company of one another. These women of color perch and step, embodying the rhythm of jazz, the exuberant chatter of the beauty salon. The muted color palette belies the exuberance of the scene, though, and hollows it. As gradient, muted, partially occluded figures unfold across the canvas, the figures reflect black fungibility less as a historic practice of thingified, commoditized exchange (under slavery) than as an ongoing process of black accumulation and degradation (throughout its afterlife). The bellies of the figures slightly protrude; their breasts subtly extend. For blackened female subjects, this bodily excess insinuates reproductive labor that implies both amplitude and exhaustion. As their singular legs overlap, commingle, and occlude the other's fragmented corporeality, the figures portray and perform a ritual of communion. Even as the figures move synchronously across a graphic visual field, their movements suggest both merger and emergence.

Disregard entails a lack of interpersonal recognition and the failure to resonate, to matter, within the social domain. *The Incognegroes* has visual, gestural, and aural components that resonate, and, in such resonance, it captures black feminine and black feminist solidarity. Of resonance, Imani Perry writes: "Both technically and metaphorically, resonance is how reverberation moves something or someone else; it is how guitar strings on one guitar respond to the plucking on another as the air between them moves, and trembles, too. Resonance is not the same as the acquisition of knowledge or the repetition or recounting of a shared experience. It is the testimony that makes another tremble, as well; that moves you and therefore shapes both feeling and thought."[41] For Perry, resonance creates harmonious stirring. It moves on lower and higher frequencies. It is the barely discernable beat that conjoins and choreographs. In resonance affect is transmitted below the skin and surface. It is sensation that alters the entire sensorium and finds its way to inner things. Resonance is the gathering of testimony and the promise of witness.

There are two participants in this poetic unfolding: two black girls turned in and toward each other. They gather in Aja Monet's poem "ree ree ree," a lyric remembrance situated in motion and in relation. Notably, even the melodic sounding of the poem's title obscures and deflects away from fixed meaning. The girls hide or hold themselves in cavernous hoods, share a blunt and exchange secrets, listen and dance to Biggie in a moment of ecstatic communion that is neither fully available nor interpretable to any reader, or onlooker, or outsider.

you my bitch, aja
crept off the smoke
from her throat

i felt honored
how we wound and heal
in the caves of our hoods
how black and brown girls
gather and peel
comparing stretch marks
and playground scars

....

how close we come to each other
never touching
how the soul
taps and gossips
the secrets we hide
under our tongues[42]

Showing one another their stretch marks and playground scars, vulnerable inscriptions of injury and imperfection, black and brown girls engage in a ritual of learning to see and heal one another. In brief rhythmic lines, the poem conjures this education and, in so doing, portrays and performs their ritual of communion. The gathering of girls is for Monet simultaneously an intersubjective and social practice that holds black women individually and collectively in a space of regard. Togetherness is thematized as the blueprint for how black and brown girls endure, sometimes with joy.

Notably, the girls' union is imperfect and, like all unions, lacks the guarantee of permanence. Nonetheless, it constitutes a relational modality that is expansive, elastic, and enduring enough to hold the quotidian injuries of twoness—and, further, of an imposing, murderous world. In her poetic practice, Monet celebrates the astounding and the everyday maneuvers of black endurance, black loss, black exuberance, but her verses lean away from any potential objectifying or usurping gaze. On the page—if nowhere beyond it—smoking, swaying adolescent black girls are protected. They keep the secrets of themselves to themselves, stowed in cavernous mouths beneath thick tongues. The only dialogue in "ree ree ree" that the reader may overhear is an affirmation of belonging, one girl telling the other: you are mine—"my bitch," my ride-or-die, my girl, my sister, my friend. (And even this the reader might not understand.)

Black Hollows alter temporalities and geographies. Given the inherent temporariness of their use, Black Hollows transform sites of containment into passageways. Corners, caverns, and crevices become the material hiding or metaphorical hidden places that facilitate concealment and escape, respite and rejuvenation, thought and sometimes touch for hollowed-out black people. These interior sites alter landscapes of domination by sequestering black subjects from the invasions of an always racialized publicness and from the never-ending risks of surveillance, pursuit, and capture that structure these landscapes. Aesthetic encounters are occasions and opportunities for reckoning. Across expressive genres, Black Hollowness is signaled by the aesthetic object's escape, concealment, or turn away from traditional, politicized modalities of black representation and from institutionalized knowledge regimes that subtend the critical enterprise. The reading practice advanced as part of my conceptualization of Black Hollows / Hollowed Blackness is one that divests from commitments to representational politics and their concomitant objectifying, if sometimes sympathetic, interpretive gestures. I am guided by Denise Ferreira da Silva's attunement to the radical potential of racially (and sexually) subordinated black female subjects who, while neither embodying nor exercising sovereign agency, can nevertheless throw entire systems of signification into peril. Black girls and women,—across gendered embodiments and expressions,—are subaltern subjects who inhabit multiple unstable identity categorizations. In avant-garde black texts, they embody modes of being that instantiate formal disruption, spatial reconfiguration, societal refusal, and living rebellion. Honoring and following them, then, Black Hollows disavow any sustained attempt at capture, reckoning instead with black femaleness as a category of critique, of excess, of undomesticated gender, and of wayward, fugitive blackness. For it is within black girls—and specifically within what fascinates and thrills them (of the low and the loving)—that we may find horizons of black livability.

3

BLACK CACOPHONY

In the face of murder, "literature" was powerless....
The Catastrophe cannot be contained in stories.
—MARC NICHANIAN

Since speech was forbidden, slaves camouflaged the word
under the provocative intensity of the scream.
—ÉDOUARD GLISSANT

Listening implies a desire to surrender.
—JOHN KEENE

BEFORE THE BEGINNING

In the penultimate scene of Toni Morrison's *Beloved*, black women gather, and they cry, screech, and holler. Responding to Denver's appeal on behalf of her mother, who is rocked nearly to death by Beloved—the embodiment of all that is disremembered and unaccounted for in New World slavery—the women arrive to rescue Sethe. Leading this cadre of black women healers is Ella. Though a seemingly minor character, Ella holds crucial significance in the novel. She, along with Sethe, commits child murder. Whereas Sethe uses a saw, Ella withholds her breast, a form of sustenance that had been instrumentalized by consumptive slavery, as lactating enslaved women typically nursed all children on the plantation, black and white alike. Ella's refusal to nurse her newborn, to whom she refers as "a hairy white thing," stunningly reverses the theft of Sethe's breast milk by the white men of Sweet Home.[1] Whereas Ella's commission of infanticide instantiates a refusal of her sexual and reproductive labor, Sethe's infanticide instantiates a refusal of racialist disciplinary knowledge. Of all her experiences in slavery, what Sethe finds most intolerable, what motivates both her escape and child murder, is the scientific authority that fragmented her people into a taxonomy of human and animal parts. Despite years spent in grief and isolation following infanticide, Sethe declares triumphantly, "I took and put my babies where they'd be safe.... Schoolteacher ain't got 'em."[2] Notably, the signifier *schoolteacher* designates a character, a civic function of the white supremacist episteme, and a principal agent in its disciplinary transfer. Sethe prefers death for her children to their surrender and service to the evidentiary metrics of nineteenth-century pseudoscience and their (quite literal) dehumanization and distortion via the slaver's *word.*

This penultimate scene of *Beloved* doubles back to its primal scene to imagine a beginning that is alternate and anterior to the beginning of things. "The Slave Trade came through the cramped doorway of the slave ship.... The only written thing on slave ships was the account book listing the exchange value of slaves," writes Édouard Glissant.[3] Insinuated in Glissant's observation is the dangerous intersection between white discursive authority (rendered with presumedly indisputable arithmetical precision and scientific formality) and black commoditization. Racial slavery ushered into the modern era the interlacement among white logocentrism, global capitalism, and black fungibility and utility (unto death). The primal scene in *Beloved* instantiates Glissant's contention that the only written things on the slave ship were ledgers recording the exchange value and the quantified rates of life, sustenance, disease, and death of its human cargo: "Ten minutes for seven letters... that for twenty minutes, a half hour, say, she could have had the whole thing, every word she heard the preacher say at the funeral (and all there was to say, surely) engraved on her baby's headstone: Dearly Beloved. But what she got, settled for, was the one word that mattered."[4]

Sethe exchanges her biogenic vitality to have the word *BELOVED* inscribed on her baby's headstone. Sharon Patricia Holland writes of the "ironic bartering system Sethe uses to purchase her baby's headstone," noting that "Sethe's body becomes the exchange for letters of a language whose words and logic have separated her from the category of human being and posited her body as a commodity."[5] Those ten dreadful minutes in which Sethe trades her sex, attention, body, and labor with a white engraver for the inscription of a seven-letter word is a stunning reversal of the biblical word becoming flesh. Evoking *dearly beloved*, a descriptor of the dead baby's (relational, as opposed to market) value *and* the phrase with which marital and funeral rites commence, Sethe's sexual commerce is a poignant, if horrific, literalization of the quintessential speech act.[6]

To be sure, this scene reflects the performativity of discourse and the violence of racial inscription, but it does not reveal fully the violence of embodied black enslavement. For New World black subjects descended from the Middle Passage, what remains of and replaces a narrative of origins and a philosophy of black living in the ruinous aftermaths of New World slavery is a legacy of indecipherable sounds—or what Junot Díaz calls "the screams of the enslaved,"[7] and Toni Morrison calls "the roaring of the people of the broken necks, of fire-cooked blood and black girls who had lost their ribbons."[8] Like the bark of Ovid's Hecuba, these sounds mark the irrevocability of loss for New World black subjects and name, in the absence of all suitable names—harms that can never be remediated.

In *Beloved*, it is Ella who survives what Morrison calls "the lowest yet" of embodied black slavery. Morrison writes:

> Ella had been beaten in every way but down. She remembered the bottom teeth she lost to the brake and the scars from the belt were as thick as rope around her waist. She had delivered but would not nurse, a hairy white thing, fathered by "the lowest yet." The idea of that pup coming back to whip her set her jaw working, and then Ella hollered. Instantly the kneelers and the standers joined her. They stopped praying and took a step back to the beginning. In the beginning there were no words. In the beginning was the sound.[9]

Ella proclaims that she has seen it all: the torture, mutilation, rape, and murder of slaves. But none of these horrendous and, unfortunately, commonplace atrocities on the slave plantation compare to the repeated sexual torments she suffered as the enslaved captive of a white man and his son.[10] Insinuated but never fully narrativized in the ominous invocation of "the lowest yet," Ella's wounding is implied by a brief catalog of objects and outcomes: missing teeth, a dead baby, a brake, a rope. These textual fragments lean on the erotic imagination (or potential sadism) of the reader to embellish what the catalog of items withholds. Despite the promise of neo–slave narratives to produce hitherto unelaborated elements of racial enslavement through historical revision within the imaginative terrain of literature, *Beloved* here recoils. Morrison's textual gesture, her provision of a mere list where the reader expects a background story, is performative of linguistic and literary limits. The practices of New World slavery, Morrison's gesture implies, were too world shattering, too mind splitting, for discursive capture or intelligible communication, even in the virtuosic text of a literary genius and Nobel laureate. So, when the formerly enslaved townswomen of Morrison's novel gather in the yard of Sethe's home to rescue her from the consumptive encroachments of plantation injuries without names, to memorialize their own losses and miseries in captivity, to sound a collective lament for the ruined world, and to summon the entire witnessing cosmos to behold it, they do not speak. They howl.

In her landmark essay "Speaking in Tongues: Dialectics, Dialogics, and the Black Woman Writer's Literary Tradition," Mae G. Henderson theorizes the significance of black women's howling in Morrison's writing. She posits:

> Howling, a unary movement of nondifferentiated sound, contrasts with the phonic differentiation on which the closed system of language is based. Like the birthmark, which is the symbolic sign of life, the howl is the first sound of life—not yet broken down and differentiated to emerge as intersubjective communication, or discourse. The howl, signifying a prediscursive mode, thus becomes an act of self-reconstitution as well as an act of subversion or resistance to the "network of signification" represented by the symbolic order.[11]

Reading Morrison's *Sula*, Henderson foregrounds the howl in part to develop a wide-ranging hermeneutic for interpreting black women's literary voices. Observing the general invalidation of black women's perspectives and experiences, Henderson critiques the subordination of black women's voices within orders of authorized speech. She argues that—to counter such invalidation and subordination—black women novelists have developed narrative strategies that recognize, interiorize, and privilege the voices of socially subordinated, politically neutralized subjects; literary practices of interlocution, dialogism, and intertextuality comprise the core features of black women's writing. Henderson draws on the biblical notion of "speaking in tongues" to theorize these practices and to develop a corresponding (black feminist) interpretive practice. As a critical concept, "speaking in tongues" exalts black women's impenetrable speech, or sounding off, beyond the patriarchal, white racial symbolic order. "Speaking in tongues" registers at once the diversity of multiple, if lost or subsumed, languages and the sacredness of divine communication; it venerates the unintelligible soundings of black worshippers to the level of prophesy. The evocative, dissonant sounds of black women, whether in their worship or literature, defy the symbolic order, which is defined by the subject's formal acquisition of language and her concomitant adherence to the rules of discourse, self- and social control, (inter)subjective and societal orderings, and the law.[12] Howling is a communicative modality that troubles the linguistic order, an affecting and affectable vocalization that announces the existence—the presence and sentience—of entities whose fealty to the symbolic order is neither established nor in evidence. In the story-worlds of African American writers, the howl is resounding, elemental, intrusive, textual proof of black life that has been abused, debased, and abandoned.

At the edge of discourse, or in its exhaustion, are the echoes and resonances of form. Inspired by the howling of Morrison's cadre of black women healers, the current chapter puts forth a theory of Black Cacophony as an aesthetic of noise *within* language, at its limits. I examine depictions of screaming, wailing, blabbering, moaning, howling in historically charged and racially inflected black texts of willed linguistic and narrative incoherence. What I am after is a theory of loud, interruptive, black textual sonicality that elaborates Édouard Glissant's observation that sentient sound does not necessarily precede or anticipate linguistic communication but, rather, sutures, supplements, and supplants it. "Since speech was forbidden," Glissant contends, "slaves camouflaged the word under the provocative intensity of the scream. No one could translate the meaning of what seemed to be nothing but a shout. It was taken to be nothing but the call of a wild animal. This is how dispossessed [hu]man organized his speech by weaving it into the apparently meaningless texture of extreme noise."[13] Black sentient sound displaces the word as the most suitable and efficacious register for expressing grievance *and* desire. A mode of semiotic subterfuge, the scream is a tactic of simultaneous revelation and reticence: it intrudes, withholds, escalates, and expires. Nonetheless, despite its ephemerality, *in its capacity to camouflage the word*, the scream has the capacity to confound systems of meaning.

Black Cacophony is a tactic of textual representation that marks both the insufficiency *and* the superfluity of language for capturing exploited or discarded black life—for example, from inside the slave ship, the detention center, the supermax prison, the plantation—while insisting, in its sentient soundings, that these lives matter. It is an aesthetic modality that refuses the domestication of history, the human, and narrative itself to the paradigm and the prospect of remote readability. In frequencies that overwhelm, throttle, and transcend corporeal surfaces, spatiomaterial emplacements and juris-political procedures, Black Cacophony transmits affects and alters cognition and judgment. In so doing, it refutes the prevailing logocentrism of Western knowledge regimes, which presume that when the wail does not eventuate in a word, human presence and intelligence are not in evidence.[14] As an aesthetic mode and a writerly technique, Black Cacophony challenges fundamentally the notion—prevalent in literary, psychoanalytic, and political theory—that egregious harm caused by interpersonal and/or political violence entails a regression to a prelinguistic state from which narrativization rescues the suffering subject.[15] It rejects the model of political subjectification that favors reasoned discourse over revolution.[16] For subjects who have surrendered the dream of legal recognition and political rescue, it effectuates (in the definitional sense of operationalizing force in the world) in a register of unfiltered and unfettered sounding (off).

Understood here in terms of both of its definitions—as a discordant mixture of sounds or noise, and as a literary device—Black Cacophony communicates hurt and want in a textual mode that eschews and exceeds discursivity. The opening of this chapter examines Black Cacophony as the practice of textual noise(-making) that dismantles the binary—posited in philosophy, literature, and political theory—between speech and silence, between (self-) representation and (self-ab)negation. Returning to antebellum slave narratives, I aim to mitigate the dividing line between and among politicized articulation; invasive, unintelligible soundings; and philosophies of the unsaid. The chapter then elaborates the uses of Black Cacophony in recent black cultural expression. It proceeds through a contemplative perusal of moments in multigeneric, multimodal texts by Alexis De Veaux and Harmony Holiday, and it explores how Black Cacophony conveys the rich, if pained and chaotic, psychic landscapes of black people debilitated by racist (structural, sociopolitical, environmental, material) ruin. The chapter concludes with a final consideration of how Black Cacophony records despair and potentiates release, resistance, and (frail, always temporary) repair. As an aesthetic mode, Black Cacophony alludes to events, actions, and emotions that subtend and animate stories but can neither be contained nor fully revealed by them; it illuminates the ways in which evocative, discordant sound exposes the affective dimensions of black experience while complicating racial epistemologies and conventional narratives of racial harm. Black Cacophony is, in essence, a strategy of literary textuality that exemplifies how language, when divested of its primary purpose of communication, is objectified and made available for both scrutiny and imaginative design.

SONIC SUBSTANCE

The deployment of Black Cacophony to index the indescribable while, paradoxically, expanding the communicative repertoire of black expressive texts and black political tracts dates back to the antebellum period. In an 1847 lecture, William Wells Brown, the prolific African American author, abolitionist, and orator, conceded, "Slavery has never been represented; Slavery never *can be* represented."[17] Brown thus articulates the central problem that has haunted North American narratives of black experience for the past two centuries—that is, at the center of African American history, where being and meaning and action should originate, is a horrific and impenetrable howl.[18] I do not make this claim to counter the central achievement of antebellum slave narratives of (1) entering the monumental catastrophe of slavery into the (predominantly English) system of discursive signification and literary dissemination; of (2) presenting incontrovertible proof of the humanity of the enslaved by configuring black subjectivity within Enlightenment protocols of, for instance, reason, literacy, autonomy, civility; and of (3) delineating a distinct genealogy of black life and being in this New World that would become the cornerstones of black culture and the (inter)disciplines that have emerged to study it.[19] Rather, I make this claim to suggest that, even as authors of antebellum slave narratives published first-person accounts of enslavement to document its criminality and to demonstrate their humanity, they recognized that the immensity of that criminality and of the suffering it caused was ungraspable by either cognition or any linguistic economy of representation. Black Cacophony is the signal of that ungraspability and the mark of the unsaid.

Subtending the modern atrocity of racial slavery was the discursive manufacture of race within the fields of philosophical and scientific inquiry. In critical black feminist scholarship spanning the past three decades, scholars like Hortense Spillers, Denise Ferreira da Silva, Michelle Wright, and Sylvia Winter have excavated the racial underpinnings of Western thought and liberal configurations of the human. They have documented, for example, the idea of the black as infantile and incapable of objective or abstract reasoning in Hegel, as preternaturally frightening and hideous in Burke, as primitive and lacking sentience in Nietzsche, and as destined for extermination in Darwin.[20] Following the Enlightenment, which generated coterminously the universal rights of Man and transatlantic slavery, scientific reason and a racialized scale of human becoming, the logos implied by speech amounts to the coextensive representation of the world and one's rightful place in it.

Western speech normativizes, that is, human agency and rationality within a totalizing, hegemonic, antiblack global order.[21] Black Cacophony, in the sound of wails, shrieks, and moans that pierce the contours of US literary texts, challenges the discursive authority of those who have arranged the world with black people at its bottom.[22]

In order to incorporate such resistant aurality within narrative schemas, authors of that inaugural genre of black self-presentation in print, the antebellum slave narrative, have tended to convert the scream into a song. To be clear, by making this assertion and pursuing its implications, I do not mean to rehearse the predominant critical practice of theorizing black literary culture in terms of black musical forms. African diasporic literary innovations—including improvisatory diegetic structures, polyphonicality and a multiplicity/diversity of narrators and perspectives, the incorporation of vernacular grammars and cultural references, and the required call-and-response of readerly engagement—have led in much scholarship to comparisons with blues, jazz, and hip-hop.[23] Undertaking a departure from this predominant critical trend, I advance here a theory of literary aurality that does not make black musicality but raw and inarticulate black pain (and sometimes) pleasure the inevitable foundation of black literary aesthetics. I engage Fred Moten's project of conceptualizing "a radically exterior aurality that disrupts and resists certain formations of identity and interpretation by challenging the reducibility of phonic matter to verbal meaning or conventional musical form."[24] What distinguishes music from "radically exterior aurality"—or cacophony—is less its presumed beauty than its presumed orderliness, and the transmission of meaning that orderly arrangements typically imply.

Despite its reference to songs, the discussion of narratives of slavery that follows concerns not so much how black literary form was made musical but, rather, how the scream has been made audible *and interpretable* in literatures of black enslavement. Readers may recall that infamous and inaugural scene of subjection in Frederick Douglass's 1845 autobiography, *Narrative of the Life of Frederick Douglass*. It is not merely the primal scene of the most prominent, widely read, and thoroughly canonized text of antebellum African American narratives of slavery; it is, more profoundly, the inaugural scene in American letters to reveal black becoming as a violent rupture of cosmological, symbolic, social, and discursive order via the extractive and hyperviolent regime of racialized human enslavement.[25] When he was a child, Frederick Douglass often woke to "the heart-rending shrieks" of his aunt Hester, who was forcibly undressed, hung, tied, and whipped. Douglass describes the beatings as for him "the blood-stained gate, the entrance to the hell of slavery."[26] I have argued elsewhere that these sexualized beatings conjure the interracial rape of which Douglass was born, as well as the violent reproduction of enslaved, captive labor through *partus sequitur ventrem*, the law that established slave status according to matrilineage.[27]

Douglass discovers "the pathway from slavery to freedom" by learning to read *The Columbian Orator*, a nineteenth-century literacy textbook that contained essays on revolt, Republicanism, and universal human rights. This is, thus, his dilemma: in his 1845 *Narrative* and its two subsequent revisions, language and literacy mark the transition from a maternal legacy epitomized by the indecipherable, heartrending shrieks of slave rape and (re)production to a legacy of possessive individualism epitomized by the discourse of democracy.[28] Because Aunt Hester's cries signal the disfigurement of the human into a thingified, exchangeable, raced-sexed commodity, Douglass must transcend the textual record of pained black noise to create the narrative of the formerly enslaved subject who can be said to have a "life"—that is, to be deserving of life and general conditions of livability. The wails and moans of sadistically abused and violated enslaved women index the brutality of bondage, vocalize the anguish of bodily and geographic dispossession, and decry the awful predicament of social death. Language here indicates the reverse (or potential reversal), rending a narrow passageway (back) into the realms of being, politics, and civility. Literacy, furthermore, instantiates the qualification of formerly enslaved black people for human recognition and for the legal entitlements of citizenship.

Saidiya Hartman and Stephen Best's essay "Fugitive Justice" might be read as a meditation on reparations for African American descendants of racial slavery. At the heart of their examination is a central query about whether the immeasurable injustices of the Middle Passage and generational black enslavement can ever be apprehended, documented, and, finally, redressed. Their query is pursued by probing the relations among narrative (or the articulability and proper ordering of injury and chronology), world-historical antiblack oppression, and liberal humanist frameworks for justice. They consider three different case studies, or three specific instances, in which appeals on behalf of the enslaved and their descendants have been put forth: first, the 1787 publication of Quobna Ottobah Cugoano's *Thoughts and Sentiments on the Evil of Slavery*, one of the earliest known autobiographical accounts of slavery, published in Britain and said to be of the most politically radical ever recorded[29]; second, the concerns and activities of the Redress Project, a collective of activists and scholars of which they were members, pursuing "questions of slavery, fugitive forms of justice, and the role of history in the political present" in the early 2000s; and, finally, the National Ex-Slave Mutual Relief, Bounty, and Pension Association, an organization formed during the post-Reconstruction period whose primary goal was to secure financial relief for ex-slaves and their progeny.[30] Given this section's specific exploration of the initial deployment of Black Cacophony in autobiographical accounts of slavery, I take up briefly here Hartman and Best's engagement with the first case study, Cugoano's *Thoughts and Sentiments on the Evil of Slavery*.

It is worth noting that *Thoughts and Sentiments* does not conform to the generic conventions of the antebellum slave narrative. In fact, in the introduction to the 1999 Penguin Classics edition, Vincent Carretta suggests that Cugoano's text was not reviewed as were other contemporaneous first-person accounts of enslavement—by, for example, Charles Ignatio Sancho and Oloudah Equiano—due to its departure from the burgeoning conventions of the genre. Cugoana's text does not open with an authenticating document by a white authority figure attesting to the veracity of the events therein recounted. The biographical sketch of the author's life is brief and seemingly perfunctory; descriptions of his capture from his homeland in Ghana, his violent transport across the Atlantic during the Middle Passage, his enslavement in Grenada, and his subsequent manumission in Britain take up a few opening pages. The greater part of the book is an impassioned plea for the abolition of the transatlantic slave trade, the global prohibition of racial slavery, and the immediate emancipation of all those held in bondage in the modern world. Ronald A. T. Judy argues that Cugoano's narrative "translate[s] literacy from a sign of Reason to one of colonial annihilation" and that it is the "first [slave narrative] to use the mastery of letters explicitly to indict slavery as a perverted economic and moral order that is only one in a long list of disgraceful acts perpetrated by the Europeans against the peoples of Africa, Mexico, and Peru in the name of civilization."[31] A scorching rebuke of the regime of embodied black slavery and a powerful admonition to its practitioners, promulgators, and apologists, *Thoughts and Sentiments* takes the form of political sermon, or divinely inspired juridical appeal.

Hartman and Best begin their meditation on potential reparations for slavery with an announcement about its permanent, fundamental, irreparable harm. Insinuating the inherent failure of any juridical appeal or legal mechanism of redress, they pose the question "How does one compensate for centuries of violence that have as their consequence the impossibility of restoring a prior existence, of giving back what was taken, of repairing what was broken?"[32] Centering Cugoano's *Thoughts and Sentiments*, they reproduce in the early passages of their essay his testimony about the innumerable and unnamable atrocities that afflict enslaved captives—that is, they make space in their essay to record, to bear witness to (in an attempt to hear *and* to sound) the "lamentations of the captive, 'those crying and groaning under the heavy yoke of slavery and bondage.'"[33] Hartman and Best acknowledge the impossibility of making "visible black suffering and audible the cries" of the enslaved in literary or juridical terms, as they quote Cugoano's conclusion: "The cries of some and the sight of their misery, may be seen and heard afar; but the deep sounding groans of thousands, and the great sadness of their misery and woe, under the heavy load of oppressions and calamities inflicted upon them, are such as can only be distinctly known to the ears of Jehovah Saboath."[34] Here, Hartman and Best extend Cugoano's concession that, despite the suffering irrefutably evidenced by the cries and deep groans of the enslaved, the injustices to which those sounds of suffering bear witness exceed narrativization and quantification (i.e., both literary and mathematical accounting) in any judgment for remedy whether political, legal, or monetary. Hartman and Best underscore "the incommensurability between pain and compensation" in order to delineate the important distinctions between grief and grievance, between the expressive modalities of pain and the discursive appeal for its end or remediation.

I spend some time examining Hartman and Best's reading of Cugoano to elucidate Frederick Douglass's deployment of evocative black sound in the interest of navigating the disparate expressive jurispolitical registers of grief and grievance in his 1845 autobiography. Again, what I am after here is a case for black sentient sound, for Black Cacophony, as the foundation of black literary aesthetics. Formerly enslaved authors, who are credited with inaugurating black self-representation in print and thereby founding the black literary tradition, had to bridge somehow the distinct expressive registers of grief and grievance. Whereas Cugoano turned to the political sermon, implemented as form in his first-person narrative, Frederick Douglass turned in his *Narrative* to slave spirituals, otherwise known as the sorrow songs. He confesses:

> I did not, when a slave, . . . understand the deep meanings of those rude, and apparently incoherent, songs. . . . They told a tale which was then altogether beyond my feeble comprehension; they were tones, loud, long and deep. They breathed the prayer and complaint of souls boiling over with the bitterest anguish. Every tone was a testimony against slavery, and a prayer to God for deliverance from chains.[35]

Successively a tale, a testimony, and a prayer, the sounds of laboring, languishing slaves become for Douglass consecrated speech, as he recuperates those mournful tones into literary form. Given Douglass's own experience of enslavement, the sorrow songs should be comprehensible to him. He maintains, nonetheless, an authorial distance from them in order to elevate them as modes of prophetic communication (like speaking in tongues) and as crafted, black cultural expression. The lyrics of the sorrow songs are notably withheld from the text; they remain for Douglass and, by extension, his readers incomprehensible sonic substance. In this regard, they are not unlike Aunt Hester's screams.

Meina Yates-Richard contends that in antebellum narratives of slavery enslaved women's howling and wailing are "discursively managed," contained, and sublimated to establish a black masculine authorial voice, to figure black masculinity as the paradigmatic site of racial injury and of black subjectivity, and to systemize the innumerable and unspeakable horrors of enslavement into an ordered and readable narrative. Linking the screams of enslaved black women and the sorrow songs, Yates-Richard posits:

> While songs and cries are distinct from one another, Douglass's *Narrative* tellingly conflates songs and the sounds of black women, effectively flattening the functional differences between these sonic forms. As Douglass is among the first writers to theorize slaves' music as an act of testimony to their experiences, it is imperative to examine the relationship he constructs between Hester's scream and the slaves' songs.... Douglass imbues the songs with an impenetrable sonic authority to represent experiences of enslavement that cannot be reduced to the logic of narrative. These "incoherent" songs are analogous to Hester's scream, which contains the kernel of slave experience that blooms into Douglass's *Narrative.*[36]

Although I am guided by Yates-Richard's comparison of Aunt Hester's screaming and the sorrow songs as incoherent modes of textual aurality that remain incomprehensible within Douglass's *Narrative*, I want to read beyond their conflation or analogousness to observe what distinguishes them. Significantly, the sorrow songs *as songs* are proper and, therefore, interpretable cultural products; as aesthetic objects they constitute a reputable and reproducible form of black cultural expression. The scream, however, is a functionally resistant noise that punctuates and punctures narratives of black enslavement to imply atrocities that are beyond representational capture and aesthetic replicability. In antebellum narratives of racial bondage, Black Cacophony exposes a level of white supremacist criminality that is forever unreckonable and unredressable—beyond, in other words, retribution *and* reason.[37] Black (feminized, maternal) soundings of the immense suffering of enslaved black people remain perpetually external and unassimilable to the regulatory regimes of politics, legality, discursivity.

It is noteworthy that Douglass does not sit in humble contemplation of Aunt Hester's terrible screams, as he does upon overhearing the sorrow songs. Whereas Aunt Hester's cries are associated with racialized enslavement and the perverse exile of the black from the domain of intelligible and legally endowed human being(s), the sorrow songs embody the ardent desire of the enslaved for freedom *as well as* their potential contributions to the worlds of art, taste, and culture. Douglass abandons the screaming Aunt Hester almost immediately after the verbal display of her sexualized suffering, which operates mainly to demonstrate the abominable plantation arrangements of which he was born and must now escape. The sorrow songs constitute a mediating modality between (nonliterate/nonliterary) black sentient sound and US democratic discourse, as emblematized in *The Columbian Orator*. That is, even though the sorrow songs do not orate explicitly or coherently the experiences of the enslaved, they do register the quest for freedom that defines the ideals of national citizenship and thus create a tie that binds the moaning and wailing of the enslaved to the revolutionary rhetoric of the Republic.

Building on Frederick Douglass's incorporation of the sorrow songs in his narrative of racial slavery, W. E. B. Du Bois textually embeds the sorrow songs in *The Souls of Black Folk*, his early twentieth-century treatise on black life and antiblack racism. Du Bois opens each chapter of *Souls* with inscriptions from African American sorrow songs. Setting the songs to musical notation, occasionally in the absence of recognizable words, Du Bois asserts that the sorrow songs are the "message of slaves to the world."[38] He argues, moreover, that these mournful sounds are so rich with human yearning, metaphysical contemplation, and political significance that they bridge ancient and future time, thereby constituting a great cultural offering of African Americans to the world.

It is important to emphasize here how Du Bois foregrounds explicitly unintelligible, untranslatable sounds of enslaved black maternal figures in the making of African American sorrow songs. Wordless sound erupts in Du Bois's text in the place where his family's genealogy should be. He describes:

> My grandfather's grandmother was seized by an evil Dutch trader two centuries ago; and coming to the valleys of the Hudson and Housatonic, black, little, and lithe, she shivered and shrank in the harsh north

winds, looked longingly at the hills, and often crooned a heathen melody to the child between her knees. . . . The child sang it to his children and they to their children's children, and so two hundred years it has travelled down to us and we sing it to our children, knowing as little as our fathers what its words may mean, but knowing well the meaning of its music.[39]

What actually happened to (and in) the mind, body, psyche, spirit of Du Bois's great-great-grandmother as she was captured, transported across the Atlantic, and enslaved remains as unavailable and unspeakable to Du Bois as the indecipherable sounds she passes on as legacy. The native language of Du Bois's African progenitor is lost over generational time to the predominance of North American English, rendering her speech, song, and sound unintelligible. There is *no possibility* of recuperating her lost narrative here, as not even Du Bois's fathers know it. Substituting, then, a narrative of origins, a national language, and even a name, Du Bois *claims* instead a black maternal inheritance of incomprehensible sounds. A form of cultural currency, these sounds index the history of generational enslavement, the durability of black life beyond the time and regime of plantations, and the qualification of African-descended people for membership in what Du Bois calls "the kingdom of culture."[40]

"Black noise," Saidiya Hartman and Stephen Best assert, "represents the kinds of political aspirations that are inaudible and illegible within the prevailing formulas of political rationality; these yearnings are illegible because they are so wildly utopian and derelict to capitalism (for example, 'forty acres and a mule,' the end of commodity production and restoration of the commons, the realization of 'the sublime ideal of freedom,' the resuscitation of the socially dead). Black noise is always already barred from the court."[41]

While juridical appeals and stories of collective harm position the injured as petitioners in need of recognition and redress within established liberal, legal frameworks, the howl and the scream call attention to the defining limits of those very frameworks. The indecipherable sounds of black noise signify the monumental injury of modern slavery as well as its continuous resurgence in expropriative, lethal, antiblack, governance structures since slavery's formal abolishment. The turn to the sorrow songs in seminal texts of black literature aestheticize black sentient sound in order to elevate it to the realm of expressive culture. Nonetheless, beyond and before such elevation, Black Cacophony is interruptive sonic insurgency. As a literary tactic that enables the raw emergence and witnessing of black suffering, it pressures the empirical arrangements of narration, history, and legality. In other words, Black Cacophony trumps the narratological and juridical impositions of causality, order, sequence, and chronology. The sonic eruptions of Black Cacophony in African American literature show black people's grief (and rage, desperation, frustration, longing) in an aesthetic modality that eludes simultaneously capture in language and brokerage in law.

SONIC SIGNIFICANCE

In an essay intriguingly entitled "Freedom's Silences," political theorist Wendy Brown, following Foucault, reminds us that "speech, because it is always particular speech, vanquishes other possible speech, thus canceling the promise of full representation."[42] Despite its instrumentalization in acts of telling, speech inevitably fails to produce complete, concrete revelation. Building on this premise, Brown mobilizes poststructuralist theories of the performativity of discourse to challenge the commonplace understanding of speech as the primary metaphor and metric of personhood and political inclusion within liberal governance structures. Advancing a critique of what she calls "compulsory discursivity," Brown emphasizes the disciplinary function of linguistic orders, which establish the norms by which citizen-subjects are both regulated and excluded. Despite the emancipatory potential of speech, she warns, it carries "its own techniques of subjugation—that it converges with unemancipatory tendencies in contemporary culture, establishes regulatory norms, coincides with the disciplinary power of ubiquitous confessional practices; in short, it may feed the powers it is meant to starve."[43] To be sure, chronicles of collective injury do not ultimately upend the hegemonic order of things. As Alexander Weheliye reminds us, "The recognition of black humanity via the conduit of suffering before and subsequent to emancipation in the United States was used to subjugate black subjects in *much more* insidious and elaborate ways than de facto enslavement."[44]

Through conceptual and ocular logics of negation, blackness structures the contours of personhood and rights-bearing citizenship in the United States. Black Cacophony is a mode of literary sonicality that resists the conceptual and visual logics of racial othering by evading (dis)closure and discursive capture. "The aural aesthetic," Fred Moten teaches us,

> is not the simple reemergence of the voice of presence, the visible and graphic word. The logos that voice implies and requires has been complicated by the echo of transgressive whistle, abortive seduction, stut-

> tered leave-taking, and by the reconstructive overtones of mo'nin'. Something is remembered and repeated in such complications. Transferred. To move or work through that something, to improvise, requires thinking about morning, and how mourning sounds, how moaning sounds.[45]

For Moten, sonic substance is not merely undifferentiated traces of speech, but speech's complication, occlusion, multiplicity. Grappling with the sonic substances of loss and longing, of racial historiography and political aspiration, requires a reckoning with the coextensive intrusions and evasions of discordant sound. Following Moten's critical injunction to think about morning, about mourning, about mo'nin, this section considers the importance of *hearing* and of *contemplating* the moan. Examining cacophonous moments in experimental, polyvocal, and multigeneric texts by Alexis De Veaux and Harmony Holiday, this section pursues a contemplative heuristic to offer critical reflections on the political and ethical potentiality of Black Cacophony.

Alexis De Veaux's *Yabo* incorporates and combines elements of the antebellum slave narrative, African cosmology, historical fiction, travel writing, and magic realism in order to interrogate historical occurrences of black pasts and to offer experimental modes of representing the sociopolitical dilemmas of black life in the present. Significantly, Aunt Hester's shrieks echo throughout the text. The narrative unfolds in a series of vignettes, interspersed with poems that reflect and sharpen its major themes: the ever-haunting history of racialized enslavement, black freedom dreams and ways, black women's sex and desire, black women's queerness, and (un)gendering within black communities. *Yabo*'s formal experiments and central narrative elements insinuate a critique of progressive temporality, rooted in the Euro-American logic of modernity and the always-already failed promise of futurity for black subjects. The poems, vignettes, dialogues, and parables that comprise Alexis De Veaux's award-winning novella take place across languages and oceans, in multiple geographies and timelines. At the center of the De Veaux's masterpiece (though not to be confused with its middle) is a fable of black diaspora that aims to remediate the harms of African capture and dispersal through the aural mimicry of nonhuman life-forms.

The chapter in *Yabo* that I am calling a fable orates an alternative history of diaspora, reads as a dialogue, doubles as an originary myth, and appears on the page as a poem in free verse. It is titled "Adansonia Digitata," Latin for "African baobab tree." The characters in conversation are Eagle and Leopard. Though in this chapter they appear as animals, later on these characters reincarnate as the leaders of a maroon rebellion and, later still, as shape-shifting spirits. Now, still at home on the African continent, Eagle and Leopard travel together from the forest to the shore of the Atlantic. Marveling at the limitless expanse of Great Water, Leopard wonders anxiously about the fate of the trees. Centering the wailing and moaning of baobab trees, Eagle recalls the violent extraction of millions of people as well as natural resources from the African continent during the transatlantic slave trade. She describes the terror of human liquidation and ecological devastation.

> Deep in the bush where a scalding heat rose from Earth, the cries and screams of our humans made the trees, whose branches looked like roots upside down cry and scream too.
>
> The trees could not bear these sounds.
>
> They did not know what was happening, but they felt it was a terrible terrible. . . .
>
> Where had these humans who bartered with some of our humans come from?
>
> Surely they were not sent by the gods, because the gods did not punish their people and plants and animals without good reason. So this was proof, the trees came to believe, of the existence of another world, a dangerous world, in which the dead had not become a part of the living earth, and, refusing to metamorphose, walked about still in human form, spiteful, brutish, warlike.
>
> What shall we do? the trees asked each other because they could not stop wailing.
>
> What can we do? they lamented.[46]

The African baobab tree is one of the oldest living species of tree, native to Africa, and renowned for its nutritional benefits, health remedies, and provision of food and shelter for humans and animals alike. Eagle relates the story of the majestic, multipurpose, sheltering baobab as a tale of extinction ("They died of heartbreak") and of heroic self-expansion and exile. In so doing, Eagle provides a countermythology to European civilizational ascendancy, attributing Europe's centuries-long imperial ventures in Africa and the Americas not to advancements in science, government, technology, industry, and the like, but, rather, to its existence as "a dangerous world," whose people were like the dead "in human form, spiteful, brutish, warlike."[47] So antagonistic were these entities to the natural orders of life, to the ideas and ethics that sustain living, that they operationalized so-called revolutions in science, technology, thought, and industry to depopulate a continent, to devise a system of global enslavement of its people, and to ravage the natural ecosystems of its many regions. Decrying Euro-American knowledge formations and their facilitation of planetary harm, the trees wailed and screamed in horror and bewilderment—right along with the kidnapped Africans.

> And then [the trees] turned to Wisest. She'd said nothing all the while, stood apart, watching.
>
> Follow and protect them, she said at last to Bravest; who, no sooner, than she was told, wrenched her colossal feet from where they'd been planted deep in Earth and spun her ponderous body, with its vast and gnarled arms, in the direction of the vanishing humans.
>
> And so Bravest followed them further and further from home, as their screams became the wind that shivered through the bush.
>
> At long last, Bravest came to stand at this very shore. There was a large stone building at the end of the land, from which frightful, frightful screams came.
>
> And there was a strange hut floating not far out upon the Great Water, stealthful as Panther.
>
> And smaller ones that took out humans across to it. With sand and water between their toes, the last of home on their feet.
>
> Now the bravest of the trees became puzzled. How will I protect them, she wondered? How will I follow them from here?
>
> Then the idea came to her. Standing at the edge of her world, Bravest dropped a seed pod hanging down one of her arms to the ground, where it burst open. She gathered the glowing black seeds and flung them out into Great Water, where fish caught these seeds in their mouths and kissed them into the mouths of more fish, swimming beneath the floating hut, as it made its way to another world the other side of Great Water.[48]

Eagle describes the hybridization of flora in the Americas, itself a feature and result of the transatlantic slave trade, as an instantiation of sonic subversion.[49] Determined to continue protecting and sheltering their humans, the wailing African baobab trees follow the masses of captured Africans to the slave forts and the departing slave ships along the shore. Rooted as trees are in Earth and land-bound, the trees are stopped at the edge of water, where they transfer their seeds, like sonic emissions, to the ocean. As the fish catch the black seeds of the baobab trees and pass them along to other fish, these ancient trees, emblems of West Africa and its lifeways, undertake repeatedly the harrowing journey across the Atlantic. As African baobab trees diversify the plant life of the Americas, they transfigure its terrain, enrich its soil, and augment the sustenance of its living organisms. The fable of "Adansonia Digitata" anthropomorphizes various nonhuman life-forms to imbue the natural world with will and with ethics—of preservation and care, of nurturance and solidarity. The fable also materializes the transmission of black sentient sound through the synchronicity and tactility of kisses.

Throughout *Yabo*, Alexis De Veaux emphasizes the presence of the somatic within the sonic and the impact of the sonic on the sensorial. Her characters emit sounds to (re)claim and express possession of their bodies. *Yabo* incorporates typical elements of the novel—a narrative arc, central characters, emplotment, dialogue—while eschewing others. Within the text, multiple universes exist simultaneously, time-space dimensions are porous, characters shape-shift into other characters. The geographical expanse of the African diaspora is condensed into material artifacts that are lost and found in museums, abandoned homes, grown-over graves, and forgotten slave ships now anchored to the ocean floor. Significantly, the story's main events resist the logic of causation wherein what has happened before might explain and justify what happens now. An episodic, temporally overlapping, and decidedly nonlinear narrative, *Yabo* refuses the notion of accretive black (or human) progress. Centering instead lost objects, persons, geographies, and possibilities, *Yabo* is an abstract, aesthetically rich text that grapples with the sonic resonances of human and ecological ruin.

The chapter "Ache Now" initiates the pairing of black woman lovers, Zen, an African American graduate student, and Steeva Braille, her racially ambiguous Jamaican cultural anthropology professor. The chapter that ends their romance is "Ache Later." Steeva is a seemingly minor character, but the stirrings and griefs she causes Zen, one of *Yabo*'s two protagonists, indicate her central function in the text. *Yabo*'s interspersed and interwoven vignettes, poems, anecdotes are tied to the central theme of becoming: becoming black, becoming queer, becoming person, becoming other. As it is contingent and relational, subjectivity in this text is perpetually made and unmade. Subjectivity is not an a priori, fixed property of the self; instead, it depends on others who are neither fully knowable nor available to the subject in the first place. Indeed, the social constitution of both subjectivity and collectivity weds interminably emergence and loss. In *Yabo* loss is rendered a nearly guaranteed outcome—in the moments love is found and in the fleeting reverie of its enactment. In De Veaux's text, loved ones—like African peoples captured, displaced, and enslaved—perish or vanish unexpectedly. Partners die or disappear. Animals vie for disappearing sustenance. Trees, as shown above, lose the humans they have sheltered since ancient times. New lovers become lost lovers with startling rapidity. The recurrent lesson throughout the *Yabo* is that for black people (and perhaps for everything that lives) pain and pleasure are coconstitutive phenomena and experiences.

Zen waits two years to take a course with Steeva because she believes that Steeva's expertise in transatlantic slavery and the making of the African diaspora are central to her dissertation. On the first evening of the class meeting Steeva instructs the class in the lesson of bodily dispossession and traumatic memory by transforming momentarily the classroom into a slave ship. To simulate the Middle Passage, she conceals the windows, renders the chalkboards invisible, and arranges the chairs in the classroom so that the seated students sit with their knees and shoulders and toes touching. She disallows their speech as she handcuffs the students one by one and then disappears into the sound of crashing waves blaring artificially through a black box on the floor. "The sound of the ocean slapping the boat's hull, the creak of wood masts, and crying seagulls filled the room with monotonous racket. Professor Braille crossed the room, fading into a corner of the dark. Zen began to shiver."[50] During this first evening of class, the frightened—if enchanted—students are transported viscerally to the slave ship's hold, crossing an imaginary ocean, to the time of black disaster.

> The walls of the room fell away, and when they fell, there was the ship, the *Henrietta Marie*, carrying a different her, that was its captain, Nathanial Paynewell, through a night and a storm. . . .
>
> Captain Paynewell tried to steady himself, listening to the monstrous night, or was it day, bellowing and outraged, suffocating him. The cargo had been difficult the entire voyage.
>
> The ceremonial baths that had been enforced were supposed to induce amnesia, to amputate body from soul, but they had not worked. And below deck, his ship bred wolves hysterical with mange, and laughing, howling hyena.[51]

The watery soundscape of Steeva's classroom facilitates the Middle Passage crossing and her own temporary transmutation into the captain of the slave ship. Despite Steeva's students' docile acceptance of her alternative pedagogy, the exercise resurrects the ancestral enslaved. The captives, packed and dying in the hold of the *Henrietta Marie*, are not visualized, are not visibilized, in this scene. Nevertheless, they are conjured here, by the sounds of their suffering and their rage.

As Steeva's alternative pedagogy demonstrates, Black Cacophony gives rise to thought experiments. By rupturing perception, breaking apart prevailing epistemes, and discrediting the commonsensical and knowable, the sonic facilitates the visceral transfer of undervalued knowledges, experiences, and histories.[52] My thinking here is guided in part by Gilles Deleuze, in whose critique of Kantian common sense, which is in the final analysis a critique of position and perception, he argues that what Kant, following the entire western metaphysical tradition, theorizes as thought is actually recognition. "For Kant," he writes, "common sense is the identity of the Self in the 'I think' which grounds the harmony of all the faculties and their agreement on the form of a supposed Same object."[53] The harmony of the perceptual faculties of an a priori subject encountering an a priori object does not indicate the principle, the faculty, or the operation of thought; it illustrates the dialectic of position and perception in the act of recognition. Black Cacophony disorganizes perception, precipitating the assault on both recognition and representation that, for Deleuze, is the condition of thought. Following this formulation, thought emerges as the subject's negotiation of that which is unrecognizable to common sense. Disarticulating the known from the epistemological and discursive authority that determines meaning—the full archive of signification—is made possible during the interpretive act. And the breaking of perception is the condition for radical critique.

Zen's reaction to Steeva's instruction is unexpected. The simulated Middle Passage transport terrifies her, and her terror precipitates a temporary loss of bodily sensation, which she surprisingly enjoys. Zen shivers and giggles. After class, she lingers in Steeva's doorway, and later that night she goes dancing with friends, consumes alcohol, and feels euphoric. A week after their first encounter, Steeva offers to serve as Zen's dissertation advisor and becomes her graduate student's lover. Steeva and Zen weave sex and instruction. These two black women engage each other's bodies in voracious, prowling ways: "Then they'd make frenzied love in the kitchen, in the hallway between the dining room and the living room, on the staircase, licking the day from each other's breasts, the desire, the ache now not a boundary but a geography neither of their bodies had known before.... the ache of words, breath on wings, ache that ruptured the difference in their ages, professional status, the branched histories of skin."[54]

The urgency and the reverie of Steeva and Zen's lesbian love are notably bound and subtended by the ongoing traumas of black life in the Americas. Like their personal histories, their sex disregards the design, logic, and specified uses of domestic spatialization; the kitchen, living room, staircase, dining room floor might be repurposed at any moment for their lovemaking. Steeva and Zen's sex eradicates time. For them twenty-four hours blend into the rapturous, erotic continuity of a single night-day. Nevertheless, it does not come as a surprise in the later chapter that Steeva leaves Zen for home, for Jamaica, to care for her dying mother. Steeva's departure and the mundane reasons for it highlight the ordinariness of loss for black women and for black queer subjects. Zen is shattered and simultaneously produced—made possible, made to live—by her lover's abandonment. What she resolves to do is to accept the inevitable loss, *the inevitability of loss*, and to make love to Steeva right up until the end comes.

Alexis De Veaux's literary experiments in *Yabo* render the narrative ambiguous, its denouement indefinite, its meanings varied. What is clear, however, is that, as various characters morph, as disparate temporalities converge, as parallel universes collapse and entwine, the soundscape of the text pulsates with radical intent. It is sound, not speech, that dissolves the distinction between the self and other, between the inside and outside, and that thereby resolves the readerly problem of distance that persists beyond sympathetic identification and critical interpretation. The penetrating ubiquity of noise—its simultaneous interiority and exteriority to the subject and to signification—entails both the democratization and the convergence of perception and position.[55] As the subject and the sound collide, the very (f)act of hearing marks the subject's own constitution as contingent and transient.[56] At the same time, interpreting cacophony requires the prioritization of what is heard over what is said. Such interpretive activity demands an excess of labor, producing knowledge as a continual and experiential process that achieves neither precision nor finitude, and that admits always the possibility of interior fallacy. Notably, the title of De Veaux's novella is not a word in English and thus has no meaning in the predominant language of the text. But in Yoruba *Yabo* means both "novice" and "invaded." In Korean it means "honey." In Japanese it means "loud." In Twi it means "high praise."

> And to remember their longing for those who
> lived on and above the horizon, who
> communicated at the porous edges of the living
> and the always living,
> they passed from mouth to mouth
> the saliva of a word,
> the unbreakable thread:
> Yabo.[57]

Yabo names the various (human and nonhuman) species borne of the black seeds of African baobab trees, crossing earthly and oceanic geographies, intermingling ancient and as-yet-unknown knowledges, building sustainable ecologies in dangerous new worlds. Yabo intones the behavior of the people and trees and fish in the chapter "Adansonia Digitata"—that is, the actuation of Black Cacophony, the distress signals of the living dead, to manifest black endurance, nourishment, and protection.

Like Yabo in De Veaux's novella, there is a unitary sign, a sound, that recurs throughout Harmony Holiday's digital project "The Black Catatonic Scream." It is Maafa, and in Swahili it means "cataclysmic event," or "catastrophe." Homing in on the inadequacy of the word *slavery*, and the mischaracterization of enforced servitude as the only cataclysmic event of black life, Holiday offers an alternate mode of expression, a sounding to suggest the "abduction and slaughter" of "the African holocaust . . . [and] what actions were taken to make Blackness blue."[58] Insinuated in Holiday's critique of the dominant historical account is an acknowledgment of the regulatory feature of language, its domestication of people and history. Holiday calls for the enunciation of Maafa to acknowledge the genocidal violence that enforced and maintained the brutal traffic in African people. Slavery was not the only catastrophe of black life; there was also the (ongoing) mass murder, she asserts, "a murderousness that rides us still."[59]

Reflecting on the Armenian genocide and its aftermath, Marc Nichanian describes the unspeakability of ruination. "The Catastrophe cannot be contained in stories," he writes.[60] There is something about catastrophe, about abominable violence, about ruinous occurrence that relegates subjects to unintelligible zones of speechless terror: "They cannot recount it, they stutter, certainly. . . . They can tell it only in bits and pieces. The event has annulled in them the possibility of recounting the totality. In essence, the event is such that beyond it there remains only a speech in pieces, splinters and fragments of speech."[61]

Speech recoils from that which evades human comprehension. Muttering, stammering, groaning are traces of the unsayable and of that which has been left unsaid. These sounds record the fragmentation of speech and evidence its shattering in the face of events and experiences that it cannot hold and communicate in totality. Nichanian underscores this self-reflexive character of speech that marks its own inadequacy. Sonic surrogates—the murmur, the wail, the stutter, the moan—appear in places and moments where speech fails and departs. Since "what happened to us on those ships and beyond" cannot be articulated in speech, Harmony Holiday calls for(th) the utterance, inhabitation, and (re)possession of a sound that has no meaning in the dominant language: Maafa.

Harmony Holiday's "The Black Catatonic Scream," a multimedia digital essay that reads as a gorgeous collection of considerations. It pursues an examination of black expressive sound that attends assiduously to the collisions and fractures of speech, silence, and their supplementary sonic intrusions. "The Black Catatonic Scream" appears in the online magazine *Triple Canopy*. Founded in 2007, *Triple Canopy* fosters practices of engaged reading and thoughtful viewership in the Internet (or so-called [dis/mis]information) age. Using a model of networked production and circulation, the digital magazine produces content based on collaborations among artists, scholars, technologists, and performers, and it regularly features works of literature, multimedia essays, public conversations, and art exhibits that engage pertinent and timely themes in politics, society, scholarship, and culture. "The Black Catatonic Scream" was published in August 2020 as part of a series, "Omniaudience," that explores sonic transmission and reception. Analyzing the conditions that foster sonic receptivity or engender sonic refusal, this series promotes attentive listening and advances the pluralization and democratization of voices in the public sphere through the blending of technology and aesthetic practice.

"The Black Catatonic Scream" reads as a digital archive of contemporary black culture in sound. In prose poems, fragmented commentary, misaligned photographs, songs, tidbits of remembrance, and brief interludes of jazz and hip hop, this project brings forward and together icons of contemporary black expressive culture, including Sun Ra, Maya Angelou, Nipsey Hussle, James Baldwin, and Judith Jameson, among others. Primarily though, as I read it, "The Black Catatonic Scream" stages a conversation (in verse) between Harmony Holiday and her passed-away jazz-musician father, Jimmy Holiday, between his catatonia and her digital-visual-sonic creativity. It parses the entanglements of madness (by which I mean the irrationality *and* the rage stoked by murderous antiblackness), black poetics, and the emancipatory yearnings of those who have descended from the Middle Passage.[62] Lingering a bit with Jimmy Holiday, as figured in "The Black Catatonic Scream," this chapter concludes with a summative elucidation of Black Cacophony as the sonic registration of grief, of indignation, and of the desperate need of black people to get free.

Wholeness—whether subjective, cognitive, corporeal, or temporal—is conveyed as and through discursive coherence. The field of psychoanalysis is predicated on the notion that the fractures and injuries of the past (and the injury of pastness itself) can be psychically managed through the remedial integration of injury into the ordered arrangement of narrative.[63] The Freudian "talking cure" proceeds from this virtually axiomatic stance and grounds therapeutic practice. "The Black Catatonic Scream" harbors skepticism about the restorative efficacy, whether psychic or political, of narrativization. It celebrates instead the power of black aesthetic expression (in poetry, song, dance, gesture) to rescue broken-hearted and broken-spirited black people from the oblivion of "speechless ruins." The project documents watershed moments of silence (such as the years following Maya Angelou's girlhood rape and the beautiful visage of Nipsey Hussle in death) and of black sentient sound (such as Miles Davis screaming his voice away and Jimmy Holiday's paranoic ramblings) in black literary and musical culture. "The Black Catatonic Scream" opens with an injunction to "learn to listen" and unfolds as a meditation on black discursive refusal.

Centering black sentient sound, Holiday indicts proponents of antiblack racism in the harms that have been inflicted, which are conveyed by the mourning and raging of those who have been afflicted.[64] "For the African diaspora," she writes,

> the scream has been an emancipatory preoccupation. The more evidence we can find of our resistance in sound, in bellow, in subjection to the danger of sounding, the more redemption we pretend, even if the screaming was a helpless, pitiful response to violence and subjection.... Each fist we don't raise at corrupt authority ends up in our throats as suffocation, supplication, and the occasional moan or scream as a form of begging our own hands loose.[65]

Holiday alludes to the textual record—in slave narratives, poetry, music, political theory, literary studies—of Black Cacophonous sound, and she notes the full affective range of black sounding as it has been documented and analyzed in black expressive and political culture. From the bellowing incitation to revolt or to run to the euphoric shout of pleasure or coming together to the whimpering plea of terror or despair, evocative sounds pervade black cultural production and black political engagement. Holiday documents the importance of black sounding beyond the cultural register. Black Cacophony constitutes the soundscape and the untranslatable underpinning of radical black thought and action.

Reading in moments as an elegy for the sometimes mute and motionless father—"Why can't dad sing today, why is he silent on the couch, and comatose?.... Why is Jimmy in such suicidal distress?"—"The Black Catatonic

Scream" thematizes the fragmentations of language, psyche, and meaning that attend catastrophe. Holiday recollects, "My dad stopped speaking in intervals throughout his life, after times of heartache, seizures, music industry trauma, marital unrest, racial profiling, nervous breakdowns."[66] Jimmy inhabits, as African Americans generally do, the zone of negated freedoms; his catatonia evinces the debilitating hurt and fatigue of such an existence as well as the violence that structures it.

> Most memorably, my dad, Jimmy, stopped speaking after strapping on some of his guns, running through his mostly Jewish Beverlywood, Los Angeles, neighborhood, and informing everyone who would listen that the Nazis were coming. He warned them and promised that he would protect them. He was paranoid and broken and full of premonitions. He stopped speaking after he was taken away in a straitjacket and given electroshock therapy for that show of pathological empathy, for his paranoiac hope for community and connection, which is the deepest blues of Black life. With each bout of catatonia, my dad's spirit rested and renewed itself, then came back, leaving him even less concerned with self-censorship, even more verbose and hopeful. In his last days, he recounted stories in tongues, switching between English and the Ghanaian tribal language that he channeled from blood memory.[67]

Caught between the hope and the frustration of perpetually unaccomplished abolition (the blurring of enslavement and emancipation that defines contemporary African American life), Jimmy, in Holiday's rendering of her father, resorts to speaking in tongues. He utters and mutters—that is, makes the impenetrable sounds of otherworldly, divine communication. As he alternates between catatonic quietude and paranoid babbling, he embodies the vocal expression of liminality. By disappearing behind/into impenetrable sound, Jimmy absents himself from the conceptual and visual logics of racist structuration. In madness, he is incapacitated. As he is rendered less functional, Jimmy becomes less available for use (for subjection or instrumentalization). His failure—or refusal—to speak intelligibly, to deliver a narrative of personal and collective harm that culminates in both the grievance and the basis for his African American identity, may be understood here as resistance to discursive cooptation.[68] In the timeless wilderness and oral/aural singularity of psychosis, Jimmy becomes self-possessed, nearly free.

> We knew things that were nobody's business. Poetry and song are forms of that catatonic tendency to use words to declare forbidden narratives,

> to lead them down a lane that turns meaning into pure feeling and accesses the telepathic quality of that spinning inward. If you can use language beyond its desire to curtail the imagination with sense, you can shut out any naysaying voice in the psyche; you can kill off your weakest alter egos and integrate yourself in the wild nonsensical where all epiphanies reside and go to hear themselves born eternal.[69]

For Jimmy, as for black subjects in general who have surrendered the dream of legal recognition and political rescue, Black Cacophony effectuates (in the definitional sense of operationalizing force in the world) in a register of unfiltered and unfettered sounding (off). Black Cacophony registers the emotive lives of black people before affect is converted into the recognizable signal of narrative *effect*. It is an insertion *and assertion* of the past into a future that is not yet foreclosed by the telos of narrative form. Jimmy's repurposing of language "beyond its desire to curtail the imagination with sense" subverts its communicative function. The brilliant, if incoherent, verbosity of his rambling is a form of black poesis in the making that opens language itself to interpretive indeterminacy and imaginative design.

In a public conversation cleverly entitled "The Sound of Getting Out," sponsored by the Omniaudience series, Harmony Holiday and Lynnée Denise discuss, via conjuration of Fred Moten, the relation of black sound to fugitivity. Holiday asks, "What are the acoustics of getting the hell out of here? How is that going to sound?" Denise responds and reiterates, "What is the sound of getting the fuck out of here? That's actually—that's the sound right there."[70] The two black women laugh. In many ways, this chapter's theorization of Black Cacophony—as an aesthetic mode *within language, at its limits*—aims to address this very question. Black Cacophony is an abstract modality of expression that conveys in narratives of quotidian black life the inevitable, ineffable entwinements of desire and disaster. As Marc Nichanian writes, "The Catastrophe is expressed fugitively."[71] The scream, the moan, the wail, the babble are resistant modes of communication. Aesthetic, and specifically textual, irruptions of Black Cacophony sidestep ritual enactments of disparate power in emotive praxes of sonic insurgency. We can hear black liberatory possibility, of the sort pursued by fugitives and runaways, in the underbelly and overtones of the scream's propulsive, provocative dissonance.

4

THE BLACK ECSTATIC

Queerness is a structuring and educated mode of desiring that allows us to see and feel beyond the quagmire of the present.
—JOSÉ ESTEBAN MUÑOZ

Somewhere, somehow something was lost, but no story can be told about it; no memory can retrieve it; a fractured horizon looms in which to make one's way as a spectral agency, one for whom a full 'recovery' is impossible, one for whom the irrecoverable becomes, paradoxically, the condition of a new political agency.
—JUDITH BUTLER

The way forward is with a broken heart.
—ALICE WALKER

TIMELESS

It is standard practice for vulnerable, multiply minoritized people to organize intellectual and political work around a theme of recovery, of regaining what has been taken, of reinstating a former position of wholeness, of reclaiming a former status of wellness. A subtle progressivist narrative underlies the notion of a future in which things are better, a politics of deferral that believes that what will come next will be constitutively different from what has come before. José Esteban Muñoz's description of queerness as a form and practice of desire that imagines (subjective, psychic, and sociopolitical) possibilities in a spatialized moment that extends beyond the present is generally understood as an ideological investment in futurity—as the political push of desire's fulfillment onto the space of the horizon. Muñoz writes:

> Queerness exists for us as an ideality that can be distilled from the past and used to imagine a future. The future is queerness's domain.... The here and now is a prison house. We must strive, in the face of the here and now's totalizing rendering of reality, to think and feel a then and there.... Queerness is essentially about the rejection of a here and now and an insistence on potentiality or concrete possibility for another world.[1]

Imagining queer futures, imagining the time of queerness *as* the future, and imagining futurity in the rhetorical, affective, and political register of queerness gets us, according to Muñoz, beyond the "quagmire of the present." By figuring the future as both the proper and ideal domain of queerness—that is, of desiring and existing otherwise—Muñoz marks the spatiotemporality of the present as the realm in which the of the violences of the past are figured and localized but persist in ways that feel permanent. The present, *here*, in Muñoz's formulation, assumes the site-specificity and concreteness of the prison, a metaphor for manifold and proliferating harms. And the present, *now*, is figured as the realm of confined thought, desire, and potentiality.

However, Judith Butler queries the "presumption that the future follows the past...... and that the future is the redemption of the past."[2] For Butler, the events, losses, and injuries of the past are themselves irrecuperable and elusive, despite their persistence in the present. The past marks the time and space of the now by virtue of its spectrality, its being both *here* and *not-here*. Moreover, Butler frames the future as a fractured horizon where the losses of the past are always contained and carried forward. A persistent and always-already impaired futurity mitigates against the notion of a future in which subjects, conditions, and life chances get better. The "quagmire of the present" is thus filled with the losses of what is now legacy, the ongoing difficulties of the immediate and everyday, and the yearning, always propulsive, that moves us beyond, if not toward, the future. The critical and political task at hand, then, is to imagine a beyond that is not temporal—that is, not future directed—but, rather, a beyond that reaches in and reckons with the ruinous now as the site of regenerative capacity and of renewed political agency. The black queer attachments, affective dispositions, political aspirations, and representational practices that punctuate the awful now with the joys and possibilities of the beyond (of alternate worlds and ways) are what I theorize in this chapter as the *Black Ecstatic*.

My conceptualization of the Black Ecstatic as an affective disposition, relational ethic, and aesthetic mode proceeds with Muñoz's caution and builds on his alternative framing of the queer beyond as (the site and experience of) ecstasy. Muñoz warns that settling with "the pleasures of this moment" imperils and impoverishes queer of color political desire and activity.[3] To conflate the trajectory and outcome of desire with mere enjoyment or accomplishment minimizes the potential of desire to serve as a resource for sociopolitical transformation. To confine sociopolitical transformation itself to futurity, to the temporality of linear progress, carries the same risk. "Take ecstasy with me," Muñoz asserts, "becomes a request to stand out of time together."[4] Ecstasy connotes a queer of color beyond that is simultaneously atemporal and communal. Muñoz posits: "Queerness's time is the time of ecstasy. Ecstasy is queerness's way."[5] Ecstasy is not mere pleasure, nor is it inevitably or even necessarily sexual. Ecstasy exceeds pleasure and sex. More important, it resists the logics of teleological progression by opening an immediate space of relational joy for black and brown people, for whom the future is both yet-to-come and already past.

The political import of the Black Ecstatic thus resides in the understanding of the time of black life as regressive and recursive. The twenty-first century marks the future tense of black liberation struggles in the United States and throughout the black diaspora—for abolition, desegregation, decolonization. The twenty-first century also follows their achievement, as the civil rights movement purportedly resulted in African Americans' attainment of true, unfettered equality before the law. The postracial era heralded and symbolized by the nation's first black presidency was supposedly indexical of the final remediation of the ongoing atrocities and legacies of transatlantic slavery and evidence of the ultimate bestowal of unqualified citizenship rights to black Americans. Nonetheless, alongside Barack Obama came the birth of the Tea Party; the resurgence of right-wing, white-supremacist political conservatism; intensified racialized, economic precarity; militarist and carceral terror-making in black and brown communities in the nation and across the globe. The awful now that has been manufactured by lethal, carceral, control governance in the United States has created an environment in which anxiety, grief, dread, not excitement or anticipation, have become the predominant affective orientations of black Americans toward the future. The third decade of the twenty-first century has witnessed a global pandemic and the alarming constancy of ecological disasters within and beyond geopolitical borders. In the United States, the third decade of the century began with the seizure of the US Capitol by white nationalists seeking to prevent the lawful transfer of presidential powers, and it has been punctuated by the repeated (media-circulated, viral) police murders of black people in their homes and throughout the expansive carceral geography that constitutes the nation.[6] In the twenty-first century, we who are black find ourselves simultaneously post-free and not yet free.[7]

In the previous chapter I theorized Black Cacophony as an insurrectionary expressive technique that indicates in black literature the unnameable and unanswerable crimes of racial subjugation, immobilization, removal. As it unfolds in this chapter, and as practiced by black queer cultural producers, the Black Ecstatic is an aesthetic performance of embrace, the sanctuary of the unuttered and unutterable, and a mode of pleasurable reckoning with everyday ruin in contemporary black lives under the strain of perpetual chaos and continued diminishment. A post–civil rights expressive practice, the Black Ecstatic eschews the heroism of black pasts *and* the promise of liberated black futures in order to register and revere rapturous joy in the broken-down present. Notably, even as my conceptualization of the Black Ecstatic is illustrated via readings of texts that center black queer men's lives, as an affective disposition and aesthetic mode, the Black Ecstatic is by no means bound or limited to them.[8] Rather, it pervades expressive forms as an abstractionist practice of conjuration that foregrounds the importance, the timelessness, and the exuberant pleasures of black communion.

In two subsequent sections, I outline my conceptualization of the Black Ecstatic. In the next, I interrogate realist representation and recognition politics as the continued bases for black media/filmic representation in the post–civil rights era. I take seriously the limits of visibility politics under the sociopolitical economy of death undergirding politically and commercially driven mass surveillance and mass incarceration in the twenty-first century. Analyzing the 2016 film *Moonlight* as a breathtaking cinematic experiment whose formal elements exemplify the Black Ecstatic, I show how this aesthetic mode illustrates an alternate means of reckoning (both affectively and aesthetically) with the manifold racialized harms that confine and curtail black lives in the period after the civil rights movement. To center experimental aesthetic practices as a viable mode of social protest in black queer literary form, as reflected and enacted in the Black Ecstatic, the final section analyzes Essex Hemphill's prose poem "Heavy Breathing." Pairing black queer poetry and black queer cinema allows for a theorization of the Black Ecstatic across expressive forms and underscores its (individual, ethical, and political) prescription for willful exuberance as the enabling index of and context for black life and liberation.[9]

TO BE A MYSTERY

As do all of the abstract aesthetic modes explored in this book, the Black Ecstatic emerges from the experience of socioracial abjection and politicized racial terror. By reading the poetry of Essex Hemphill alongside *Moonlight*, this chapter emphasizes the social disasters that were heralded under the Reagan administration, including the federal withdrawal of civil rights protections, the crack epidemic, the diminishment of social support and safety for impoverished black and brown people, and the proliferation of racialized confinement. My conceptualization of the Black Ecstatic as an aesthetic mode—an innovative representational practice and textual technique that crosses the boundaries of discrete literary genres and media platforms—proceeds from the premise that representations of political crises in black life since the 1980s do not inhere in established literary or visual media forms. Rather, as forms of racialized economic, social and political harm has itself become less formal and more abstract—the move, for example, from legal segregation to segregation produced via educational disparities, deindustrialization, and redlining practices—the expressive techniques used to tell stories of black life, struggle, and aspirational freedoms have themselves become more abstract.[10]

Abstraction here connotes aesthetic modes of signification that are simultaneously nonrealist and nonfigurative. In "The Rules of Abstraction," Leigh Claire La Berge posits that abstraction both functions as a "metonym for something undefined" and "denote[s] something crucial and real that necessarily remains unexplained."[11] The abstract registers that which crucially and meaningfully exists but that nonetheless exceeds, obscures, or defies mimetic capture. Within an analytic lexicon, La Berge argues, "the abstract is employed as a trope that organizes and structures but that itself eludes definition and representation."[12] As both hermeneutic and aesthetic, abstractionism offers blackness the potential for meaning outside of the representational economies of violence and erasure that define its status in modernity. "For at stake in the 'modern,'" Lindon Barrett reminds us, "is the animation of a conceptual form—the commodity—as the principle of economic (and general) rationality, in the face of the already fully animate individual and collective forms—in human proportions—of racial blackness."[13] The collective experiences of black people in the West—which include past and present iterations of black captivity, corporeal dispossession, political disenfranchisement, economic abandonment and social disposability—is rooted in a ruthless Euro-American modernity that defines the contours of being, belonging, and becoming in racialized, monetized terms. Contemporary black queer cultural production that eschews mimesis and representational realism reflects the understanding that conjuring blackness solely within existing normative aesthetic and political representational apparatuses (regardless of how positive, authentic or real) risks relegating black subjects who are cited and sighted within blackness's domain again to the status of commodity.

Taking seriously black life as defined by the perpetuity of sociopolitical crisis, the Black Ecstatic engages liberatory modes of endurance in our broken-down but ongoing present. The Black Ecstatic ruptures, renovates, and resignifies the formal features of traditional African American protest literature and visual propaganda. Insofar as African American cultural production has historically attempted to remedy the psychosocial, material, and political conditions of black life, it has typically attempted to do so by means of representational revision or correction. Borrowing Nathanial Mackey's term "outfulness," Anthony Reed argues that experimental black writing "opens new horizons of thinking by calling into question the grounds of knowledge."[14] Black aesthetic abstraction interrogates the systems of thought, social organization, temporal schemas, and protocols of political governance and participation that define the Enlightenment's enterprise of modernity. "Outfulness," Reed suggests, "reimagin[es] the connections between race and history and stress[es] forms of nonsynchronism in the present. . . . Black experimental writing represents an instance of 'taking it out,' a practice of outfulness cast as freedom."[15] Freedom is imagined and instantiated within the fugitive modality of "outfulness," of stepping outside of progressive time and, for my purposes here, moving beyond and beside oneself in communion with another in the affective register of black ecstasy.

In the introduction to *Pleasure Activism: The Politics of Feeling* Good, editor-gatherer adrienne maree brown argues for the necessity of pleasure to support and sustain the everyday lives and emancipatory endeavors of black and brown people. She revisits and expands the concept of the erotic beyond the manifestly sexual and desirous to recognize its energetic, sensual, transformational force so compellingly conceived by Audre Lorde in "The Uses of the Erotic: The Erotic as Power," brown foregrounds pleasure in the sensorial and social realms as an essential survival resource for members of devalued, discarded populations. She explains:

> We are in a time of fertile ground for learning how we align our pleasures with our bodies, decolonizing our bodies and longings, and getting into a practice of saying an *orgasmic* yes together, deriving our collective power from our felt sense of pleasure.
>
> I think a result of sourcing power in our longing and pleasure is abundant justice.... That we can instead generate power from the overlapping space of desire and aliveness, tapping into an abundance that has enough attention, liberation, and justice for all of us to have plenty.[16]

For brown, the pursuit of erotic and/or activist pleasure is a decolonial praxis, one that privileges an abiding commitment to justice, urges the equitable redistribution of the world's resources, and honors acts of exuberant aliveness. brown's analytic of pleasure insists on reparative sociality, which may be understood as both ethical and ecstatic.

The 2016 film *Moonlight*, directed by Barry Jenkins and adapted from Tarell Alvin McCraney's play *In Moonlight Black Boys Look Blue*, deploys the Black Ecstatic substantively, symbolically, and structurally. Recalling his childhood in Liberty City, Miami, the impoverished black neighborhood in which *Moonlight* is set, McCraney claims that "some of the worst days of [his] life" also featured the most natural beauty.[17] "The poinciana would be in full bloom and falling on your head," he says, "so you'd see these yellow flowers everywhere, but, you know, I had just gotten either beaten up on a corner or saw somebody get shot."[18] McCraney draws attention to the commingling of terror and beauty in black life that so often eludes mimetic capture. After all, how does one represent in moving pictures the horrible juxtaposition of seeing the fragile materiality of the body giving way under the impact of a bullet, or the experience of assault bruising the soul alongside the vivid beauty and coming glory of Miami flowers in spring bloom? For Jenkins to tell the story cinematically that McCraney had written but not published, the deployment of experimental narrative and filmic technique was essential. As abstract aesthetics shape black cinematic possibilities, what follows is an analysis of *Moonlight* that illustrates how the Black Ecstatic undermines mimetic representation in the depiction of black queer, masculine becoming.

Even as *Moonlight* centers the development of its queer black boy protagonist Chiron, it narrates the story of a particular place and time. Set in Reagan-era Miami, the film addresses the variety of social disasters that plagued black communities. For instance, Chiron's drug-addicted mother, Paula, is emblematic of the familial and communal devastation wrought by the crack academic, the emergence of draconian "war on drugs" legislation, and capitalist-driven and racialized carcerality. *Moonlight* obliquely depicts the war on drugs as the main engine of mass black imprisonment—that is, side-stepping the grueling spectacularity of juridical procedure, carceral containment, and slow death. Counterbalancing the film's overall thematic despair is the ecstatic register of its lush color tones. Rich blues, purples, yellows, and greens insinuate a vitality that is belied by the film's predominant representation of black life, framed always by the grim specter of sudden or slow demise.

The opening scenes of the film alert viewers to the harrowing circumstances of Chiron's life, which are perilously personal and reflective of the collective precarity of black life in the post–civil rights period. Early on, a crack-addicted man pleads with a young dealer for an advance on drugs. The desperation of both the crack-addicted man, seemingly homeless and ravaged by crack addiction, and the young man, whose participation in the illicit trade provides the only opportunity for economic sustenance, is apparent. This scene is a familiar one, signaling the urban malaise that has gripped black and brown communities for decades. The familiarity of this cinematic depiction is both underscored and undercut by the arrival of Juan, the drug dealer for whom the young man works. Juan asks about his employee's mother in a brief exchange that shows his obvious regard. The insertion of care rather than cruelty, and the emphasis on economic opportunity rather than mere exploitation, marks both Juan's and the film's relational ethics. Juan's capacity for care is further evidenced when he finds Chiron, who has been harassed and chased by a group of boys for his presumed queerness, hiding in abandoned public housing. He offers the boy momentary safety and the promise of alternative family. As the film's proximal father figure, Juan feeds Chiron, introduces him to his partner, Theresa, who serves as a surrogate mother, and teaches the queer black boy important life lessons.

Played by African American and Muslim actor Mahershala Ali, Juan informs Chiron that he is Cuban, noting that there are a lot of black Cubans, though not in Miami. Juan's presence within Liberty City reflects the complicated workings of the African diaspora in Miami, in which violence, displacement, familial disruption, and poverty impact African American, Haitian, and Cuban populations alike—and in which any political vision of salvific black sociality necessitates and incorporates these diverse diasporic populations equally. The kinship arrangement that Theresa and Chiron establish as surrogate parents for Chiron reflects the alternative filial structures of both black diasporic and queer families. Juan's paternal interest and instruction open for Chiron avenues to self-love and self-acceptance. It is Juan who

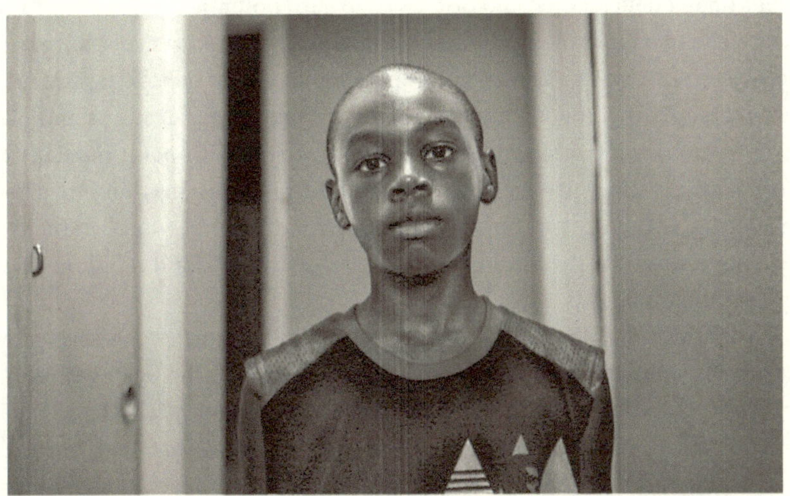

FIGURE 4.1 Still from *Moonlight* (dir. Barry Jenkins, 2016): Chiron as a child in the hallway/corridor.

shows Chiron, in two separate scenes, that, one, it is OK to be black, and, two, that it is OK to be queer. Juan, the drug dealer who sells crack to Chiron's mother and thus facilitates the destruction of Chiron's fragile family helps to raise and to save him.

Juan's ambiguous role in Chiron's life—as both source of harm and source of healing—bespeaks the dual, elemental structure of ecstasy. "The man in ecstasy and the man drowning," Kafka writes, "both throw up their arms."[19] This observation calls attention to the inexorable entwinement of ecstasy and disaster. The unruly structure and experience of ecstasy carry the risks of overwhelm and destruction, even as ecstasy eventuates in renewal after the disastrous event. Ecstasy externalizes our insides, imperils self-sovereignty, builds on felt deficiencies, and orients us toward potentially disastrous fulfillment. The term for frenzied, cumulative emotion, ecstasy evolves from the Greek *ekstasis,* which means "to be or stand outside of oneself, a removal to elsewhere." By turning us outward, ecstasy compels our gestures and pleasures beyond the containments of self and surface; it operationalizes the limit, which it also perpetually violates and reforms. Ecstasy thus emerges as an alternate structure for the black queer beyond, one not rooted in the temporal logics of futurity, but in the affective, embodied, and relational pleasures of the disastrous now.

Portraying limits that it repeatedly violates and reforms, *Moonlight*'s movie heroes are simultaneously its villains. The boy, Kevin, who brings Chiron to orgasm and initiates his queer eroticism, is the same boy who later bashes Chiron's face repeatedly in a homophobic gang beating that nearly destroys our protagonist. Despite its sympathetic rendering of black boys' incapacitated lives, *Moonlight* resists the promise of race-based sociopolitical and economic improvement. Refusing the more familiar triumphalist narrative of black male becoming, the film instead punctuates its chronicle of racial suffering and black masculine malaise with portrayals of rapturous joy. The film unfolds in three distinct parts in which the central narrative event is a mundane encounter: a swimming lesson, the first erotic exchange, a visit to an aging parent, a first date. Time passes between the three parts of the film, but the three sections neither mark nor adhere to depictions of accretive progress in the lives of its characters. In fact, the negative outcomes of such bleak social circumstances are so likely that the film neither represents nor mourns the losses when they do occur.[20] Juan, for example, dies prematurely; his death occurs entirely off-screen and is barely remarked upon by the characters. Two of the main characters, Chiron and Kevin, spend formative years in prison, but such black encounters with the carceral state are minimized. That Juan's death and Chiron's imprisonment occur off-camera evinces a mode of cinematic abstraction wherein the intimate experiences of anguish and deep grief are given not only the sanctuary of privacy but also the status of human experience that exceeds representation and representability. The film thus eschews those commonplace scenes of racial harm and racial heroism that are so typical of contemporary US cinema.

By refusing the spectacularization of commonplace black male suffering, *Moonlight* relegates scenes of racialized harm to the intimate sphere of the private. The spectacular, highly visible, and fantastical—that is, *public*—character of embodied blackness grants it a level of iconicity and, in Harvey Young's astute formulation, "a compulsory visibility."[21] Young writes: "The black body, whether on the auction block, the American plantation, hanged from a light pole as part of a lynching ritual, attacked by police dogs within the Civil Rights era, or staged as a 'criminal body' by contemporary law enforcement and judicial systems, is a body that has been forced into the public spotlight and given a compulsory visibility."[22] In the neoliberal, carceral state, African American presence and participation in the ordinary, everyday behaviors and movements that characterize civic belonging are converted into ritualized iterations of racial subordination and civic exclusion—that is, into repetitive *public* stagings of egregious, antiblack injury. The US carceral state, with its technique of hypersurveillance, embodied containment, and social removal, effectively robs black people of what Hortense Spillers has recently described as "privacy as a fundamental human right."[23] Following Spillers, I pose here a few questions: What aspects or practices of the self gather within the domain of "the private" in the formulation of privacy as a universal right to which every human has claim? What is it about the *publicness* of blackness that creates in others such false and intrusive intimacy? How might sexuality and alternative sociality provide sites of refuge and of play for black subjects? And, finally, how might we all settle more comfortably with the mystery and the complexity of human beings whose acts and inclinations do not necessarily adhere to the logics of language or the schemas of representation?[24]

The final line of Rita Dove's poem "Canary" reads: "If you can't be free, be a mystery."[25] This line encourages the practiced, purposeful confounding of representational signs. My conceptualization of the Black Ecstatic builds on the politics of opacity underlying the call of "Canary," memorializing Billie Holiday, to "be a mystery." Notably, the ambiguity of the closing scene of *Moonlight* suggests the acceptance of this call.[26] The scene, which takes place in Kevin's home, returns implicitly to the earlier domestic scene in which Chiron sits with Juan and Theresa in their kitchen. Chiron queries Juan about his sexual identity, asking, "Am I a faggot?" Juan immediately distinguishes homosexuality from the demeaning epithet but allows the possibility that Chiron might be gay. When Chiron asks when he will know the presumable truth of his sexual identity, Theresa warmly assures him that in time he "will know." However, in *Moonlight*, as in black life generally, time is not particularly productive of reparative outcomes. The film concludes by withholding such knowing from the audience, and perhaps from the characters themselves. By refusing the fixity of sexual identification, *Moonlight* registers skepticism about the presumed positive relation of sexual desire and erotic autonomy to disclosure and display. Culturally specific, Western notions of gender and sexuality as organizing features of public life and landscapes are often mistaken for universally applicable citizenship rights within neoliberal orders. For me, someone who is and was raised Muslim, the ethics of gender and sexuality, along with assumptions and aspirations about sexuality's emancipatory promise, depend on a different understanding of the boundaries between the public and private. As someone who parents a young adult African American Muslim whose racialized criminalization is pursued through hypersurveillance techniques evolved at the intersection of the war on drugs and the war on terror, I am invested in retaining spaces of license, exploration, and pleasure—or, more plainly, sites of privacy—that allow black people to experiment with undisciplined and undocumented emancipatory practices.[27] The value of privacy and of "be[ing] a mystery" undergirds the representational procedures of *Moonlight*. In his study of cinematic representations of black masculinities during the US presidencies of George W. Bush and Barack Obama, Jared Sexton critiques the redemptive arc of black masculine cinematic representation as it has been deployed as a militarist and imperialist alibi. Sexton finds in the figuration of Chiron a notable exception. "Chiron is better understood as a figure of wonder than of identification or desire," he suggests: [Chiron's] relative silence, which likely indicates both an inhibition and a protective reticence linked to severe and prolonged mistreatment, is most nearly what defines his personae across the radical metamorphosis in physical appearance, from the soft and diminutive Little to the lanky and awkward Chiron to the hardened and muscular Black. And in that silence his mind seems absorbed not so much in longing or reflection as in mystery.[28]

I am moved by Sexton's characterization of Chiron as a quiet, contemplative figure who simultaneously evokes and evades the performative and expressive codes of racialized being and (masculine-) gendered bearing. It is

Chiron's quiet inscrutability that renders mystery his most salient and stable quality across the jagged cuts of the film's tripartite narrative and the drastically different appearances of the actors who portray him. It is worth noting also that Chiron's radically altered embodiment over the course of the film illustrates the process of epidermalization as the disjunctive, if layered, accruals of meaning etched into black flesh across the life cycle.

Moreover, I find reflected in *Moonlight*'s diegetic and cinematographic techniques my own critical desire to frame black queerness not as identity or mode of desire per se but as relational ethic and site of alternative political and representational possibility. In the final scene of the film, for example, Chiron discloses to Kevin that during the intervening years he has remained untouched, that he has not had other lovers, whether male or female. Likewise, Kevin reveals details about a prior heterosexual romance and resultant fatherhood even as he carefully prepares a delectable meal for Chiron in what feels like a ritual of courtship. The film ends with a heartfelt, healing embrace between the two characters that insinuates their deep intimacy but that also resists the explicit sexualization of it. In other words, what will become of Kevin and Chiron's night in Kevin's bedroom, and of all their nights to come, remains shrouded in mystery. Mystery in *Moonlight* offers an alternate path to both experiential freedoms and abstract expressive formations.

Rather than an appeal to queer eroticism in terms (or on behalf) of black masculine subjectivities or as the guaranteed site of reparative black masculine intimacy and survival, *Moonlight* emphasizes fleeting, rapturous communion between subjects gendered black and male. Structuring the film's tripartite progression is a series of ecstatic encounters between black boys and black men who endure violent lives of rigorously imposed limitation. In *Moonlight*'s first section, two scenes that evince the Black Ecstatic follow one another. In the first Kevin encourages Chiron to defend himself against bullies who consider him "soft," a schoolyard euphemism for Chiron's apparent queerness. Challenging Chiron to demonstrate his skill as a fighter even as he helps him to develop it, Kevin hits Chiron, and the boys wrestle to the ground. The camera angle is low as the boys roll around, their bodies intermingled to the point of indistinction in the sunlit grass. As the boys pant and grunt, the effort and the ecstasy of aggressive touching is sounded. This sounding is the labored breath of black life: contained, curtailed, hovering at the threshold of death and yet persistent, resistant, ecstatic.

My attention to the sound of heavy breathing here anticipates the extended meditation and multivalent significance of that phrase in Essex Hemphill's poetry in the following section. More immediately here, Kevin and Chiron's heavy breathing reflects the "social ecstasy" that Ashon T. Crawley theorizes in *Blackpentacostal Breath*. Building on the Fanonian understanding that blackness is socially constituted in part through the stifling of breath, Crawley attends to the ambient, ambivalent (aesthetic and political) possibilities of the embodied exultation and deep breathing characteristic of ritual black communion. Such communion produces social ecstasy within and between black subjects, Crawley argues, through their "being beside oneself together with others." He asserts:

> Social ecstasy is not about the unbecoming of the subject when confronted with an Other that assumes that doneness is what exists naturally. Rather, social ecstasy is the conception that the condition of possibility for life is undoneness as ontological priority, an irreducible, unreachable doneness, a horizontal undoneness. The emptying of oneself though spiritual peregrination underscores the capacity to give and receive, to disperse and hold, and lays claim to undoneness as a way of life. . . . Social ecstasy as the emptying out of oneself toward a social produces and is produced by infinite possibility.[29]

Kevin and Chiron's wrestling match is a ritual of black boy sociality. While it anticipates their more explicit erotic encounter as teenagers on the beach, its more immediate significance is the way it figures "undoneness as a way of life." The wrestling match risks in this moment not only the boys' coming together but also their coming apart in an aggressive exchange in which one might best the other. Notably, neither Kevin nor Chiron is a fully formed masculine, sexual, adult subject; as black children, they exist rather in a state of (always racially bounded) potentiality. Their pretend battle strengthens the other for the perils that lie ahead. Their wrestling match, moreover, instantiates and further develops their ability "to give and receive, to disperse and hold" the other. Chiron and Kevin's labored breathing captures the unsayable, the inarticulable, premise and promise of the Black Ecstatic. After the wrestling match ends, Kevin extends an arm to help lift Chiron. Breaking this moment, the camera lingers on a shot of Chiron's face against the grass, his eyes and mouth softly agape, in the quiet reverie of belonging. The direction of Chiron's gaze suggests poignantly the upward motion of rapture.

Directly following the wrestling scene is the one in which Juan teaches Chiron to swim. Assuring the boy that he is there to hold and catch him as needed, Juan both substitutes for the father Chiron does not have and antici-

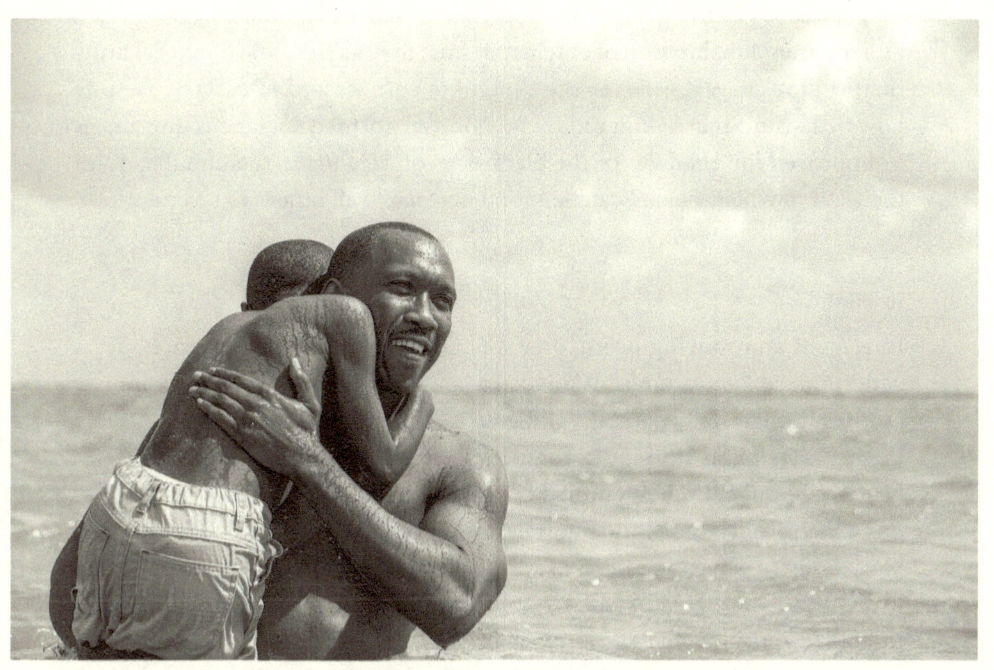

FIGURE 4.2 Still from *Moonlight* (dir. Barry Jenkins , 2016): Juan carries Chiron in the ocean.

pates the man Chiron will become. Classical music provides the soundtrack to the swimming lesson, ecstatically transporting both characters and viewers to another place *in this time*. In these Black Ecstatic scenes, black boys and men discover themselves and each other against the backdrop of sea and sky. In these moments, black male bodies caress black male flesh, black male limbs entangle, black male heads are cradled in the hands and arms of black men. During the film's Black Ecstatic moments—when Juan teaches Chiron to swim; when Kevin wrestles with Chiron; and, later, when Chiron achieves orgasm—the movie's incremental pacing slows further to the time of a caress or rushes to the pace of a sprint. These instances, notably, are marked by a different inhabitation of cinematic time; they achieve the temporal unity that Muñoz characterizes as the time of queerness and of ecstasy. Despite how little is ultimately offered by way of transformed social circumstances or improved life chances for the black boys of *Moonlight*, the film illustrates the ways in which Black Ecstatic moments enable all others to be endured.

TO BREATHE

In elegant and moving prose, poet Claudia Rankine writes of black life as conditioned by mourning: "We live in a country where Americans assimilate corpses in their daily comings and goings. Dead blacks are a part of normal life here. Dying in ship hulls, tossed into the Atlantic, hanging from trees, beaten, shot in churches, gunned down by the police or warehoused in prisons: Historically, there is no quotidian without the enslaved, chained or dead black body to gaze upon or to hear about or to position a self against."[30] The proximity to death—historically constant and sociopolitically produced, monetized and spectacularized—characterizes black life in modernity. Underscoring the ordinariness of death-producing violence visited upon black subjects, Rankine issues a warning against the traffic in its spectacle. Realist representation undertaken in protest often narrativizes black suffering and demise through the deployment of literary and visual spectacle. This predominant practice of what Lauren Berlant calls "sentimental politics" is the liberal deployment of injurious narratives to garner civic intervention and legal reparation.[31] Within the sentimental political frame and practice, recognition of group harm is understood to be the primary metaphor and measure of inclusion within liberal frameworks of personhood and of political mattering.

In her strident critique of sentimental politics, Berlant observes that even though "subaltern pain is deemed universally *intelligible*," it "is not considered universal."[32] Subaltern pain (or, following bell hooks, "racial pain") neither constitutes nor characterizes the psychic, social, and material conditions that organize the life-worlds of majoritarian subjects whose identities permit their normative abstraction and participation within liberal frameworks of democratic inclusion.[33] Racial pain is, rather, an unexceptional mark(er) of black—or, to use Berlant's term, subaltern—distinction. Berlant offers a productive caution to marginalized, minoritized subjects whose political strategies rely on publicized narratives of collective trauma: "Pain thus organizes your specific experience of the world, separating you from others and connecting you to others who are similarly shocked (but not surprised) by the strategies of violence that constantly regenerate the bottom of the hierarchies of social value that you inhabit. In this sense, subaltern pain is a public form because it makes you readable, to others."[34] Berlant critiques trauma narratives in part to distinguish the explosive but contained temporality of the traumatic event from the ongoing terrors, injuries, and aches that typify the lives of those in subjugated collectivities. She cautions that narrativized rehearsals of collective trauma unwittingly reinforce asymmetric arrangements by framing group harm within the calculable terms of the historic claim and juridical redress. Furthermore, sentimental politics demonstrate an abiding belief in and commitment to recognition and rescue within existing (legal, civic, socioeconomic, and political) givens. However, for marginalized, minoritized subjects whose vulnerabilities are compounded and whose exclusions are maintained via the schemas of epistemic and political rationality, there is far too much risk in appealing for remedy and protection from the very governance structures, institutions, ideologies, and figures from which these subjects need remedy and protection in the first place. Berlant issues the following sobering corrective: "The public recognition by the dominant culture of certain sites of publicized subaltern suffering is frequently *(mis)taken* as a big step toward the amelioration of that suffering."[35]

While Berlant's critique of sentimental politics is not aimed at minoritized literatures per se, it alludes, nonetheless, to the enduring romance of literary redemption as itself a form of social renewal. That is, her critique speaks to the belief that minoritized literatures can intervene in social problematics as repositories of truth and engines for societal change, or that subaltern speech can itself arbitrate and ameliorate material and political crises. Berlant's critique of sentimental politics and, implicitly, of a sentimental attachment to the redemptive promise of the literary enterprise might be directed at discursive representation in general. Building on a Derridean preoccupation with the interimbrication of language and law, Kalpana Rahita Seshadri states the case astutely: "Law and language are coextensive. There is no part of language that is not always already instituted, conventionalized, submitted to the protocol of the sign as representation and repetition."[36] The Black Ecstatic alludes to fractured subjectivities, the ineffectuality of progress in repetitive crisis time, euphoric silences, overlapping and disjunctive temporalities, and the perilous freedom of incoherence. By deploying textual practices of disorientation, disaggregation, and dissemblance, the Black Ecstatic intervenes at the interstices between language and law; it captures aesthetically and ethically "subaltern suffering," or racial pain, but eschews normative articulations that (re)produce such pain as already known (or *knowable*), as commodifiable, and as narratively remediable.

In the face of mass group demise, the Black Ecstatic registers a critique, if not outright refusal, of recuperative, redemptive futurity. It emphasizes instead the exuberant rapture of urgent, if fleeting, communion between death-bound (black) subjects who exist in the ongoing, awful now. It is for this reason, I believe, that the Black Ecstatic was innovated by black queer cultural producers confronting the deadly AIDS epidemic at the end of the twentieth century. Within two brief decades after the civil rights movement, the hard-won, uplift-oriented legislative and economic solutions to centuries of racial harm were being reversed. The concentration of poverty, the removal of educational and employment opportunities secured through affirmative action mandates, the crack epidemic (alongside the criminalization of addiction), and the ravages of AIDS in black and queer communities reflect the steady erosion of civil rights gains. Under the Reagan administration, the globalized outsourcing of manufacturing industries intensified poverty in African American communities. Degrading discourses about black mothering and black familial patterns and practices proliferated, enabling the withholding of basic state-based support by the federal government. Programs aimed at alleviating poverty, including Aid to Families with Dependent Children (AFDC) and affordable housing were defunded. The criminalization of black life—whether in terms of aggressive racialized policing and emergent capitalist carcerality, or the popularization of narratives of illegitimate and excessive welfare dependency by unwed black mothers—led to the widespread devaluation of black lives concomitant with reinvigorated white supremacy during the Reagan era.

In her monumental study *The Boundaries of Blackness: AIDS and the Breakdown of Black Politics*, Cathy Cohen explores how AIDS influenced black community formations and political agendas in the 1980s and 1990s. Specifically, she tracks how black leaders, politicians, and policy-makers, as well as the organizations they led, responded to the spread of the disease within black communities. The belief that AIDS mainly consumed the lives of intravenous drug users and members of the LGBTQ community slowed the development of an urgent and robust system of advocacy and prevention on behalf of African Americans. Cohen shows the incremental development of health advocacy, educational outreach, and information circulation that were used to stem its ravages. Despite the presence of African Americans in positions of political leadership and in key roles within social service organizations, the 1980s had ushered in a wave of newly repackaged and reinvigorated forms of racial containment, exclusion, and removal. It is within this context that the black gay community solidified publicly to advocate for those whose lives were ravaged by AIDS and for their loved ones. In the early years of the epidemic, the first attempts to halt the spread of AIDS, to insist on research and treatment to effectively combat the disease, to agitate for dignified health care practices, and to refuse the decimation of black lives by this disease were black gay activists. Fighting for their lives and the lives of all black and queer people, these black queer activists innovated the Black Ecstatic as a queer expressive modality that aestheticizes black mystery and synthesizes fleeting moments of black communion into an exhilarating eternality.

The Black Ecstatic offers an alternative mode of documenting, grieving, and cherishing black queer lives lost to the ravages of the AIDS epidemic at the close of the twentieth century. In *Undoing Gender*, Judith Butler unpacks the concept of ecstasy in specific relation to queer loss and grief in the wake of AIDS.[37] She suggests:

> To be ec-static means, literally, to be outside oneself, and this can have several meanings: to be transported beyond oneself by passion, but also to be *beside oneself* with rage or grief. I think that if I can still speak to a "we," and include myself within its terms, I am speaking to those of us who are living in certain ways *beside ourselves*, whether it is in sexual passion, or emotional grief, or political rage. In a sense, the predicament is to understand what kind of community is composed of those who are beside themselves.[38]

Living (and dying) beside himself in sexual passion, emotional grief, and political rage, Essex Hemphill was a poet of the Black Ecstatic. Born in 1957 to a working-class family in Chicago, he was one of five children. Hemphill experienced paternal abandonment at a young age, which informed his belief in black familial and relational formations as necessary sustenance for black queer subjects. In their settings that condense long stretches of time, in their polyphonic verse, in their complex renderings of unexpected and unaccepted desire, and in their insistence on the innate value of black queer life, Hemphill's writings provide a compelling case study of how black protest is rendered in abstract literary form.

Though he began writing earnestly at the age of fourteen, Hemphill did not disclose all of the details of his personal life in a single, simple memoir.[39] Hemphill's writings span expressive forms: essays, short stories, poems, and films. A black gay man, a fearless AIDS activist, and a poet in search of a revolution that had already failed him, he was dying as he composed his last published works. Writing during the height of the AIDS crisis, the war on drugs, and the emergent carceral state, Hemphill contended with a second nadir in African American experience. Beginning in the Reagan era, the legislative retrenchment of civil rights gains, the withdrawal of social supports through the dismantling of welfare programs, the crack and AIDS epidemics, and the mass carceral containment of black and brown people led to a contemporary period of reinvigorated black suffering that was reminiscent of the early twentieth century just as the 1990s was nearing their end.

My contemplation of black queer poetics that emerged during this period is conversant with Dagmawi Woubshet's luminous study *The Calendar of Loss: Race, Sexuality, and Mourning in the Early Era of* AIDS. In this text, Woubshet theorizes black queer expressive and political culture in the 1980s and 1990s, when AIDS had such a lethal impact on queer life that entire communities were decimated, entire neighborhoods depopulated. Coining the term "a poetics of compounding loss," Woubshet argues that black queer poets innovated insurgent praxes of aesthetic (and often political) expression that revealed and reckoned with the inescapability of disease and demise for black queer subjects. Caught in unending cycles of incalculable loss and immeasurable grief, black queer poets in the early era of AIDS endured (and mourned) the passing of leaders and loved ones in rapid succession even as they confronted (and grieved) their own anticipated deaths. As Woubshet incisively and movingly demonstrates, the psychic, emotional, and political labor of mourning was in this time coextensive with black queer living. Woubshet observes poignantly that the interimbrication of life and early death, of sorrow and stigma, and the political insistence on otherwise typifies black existence generally. "The paradigm of black mourning," he writes, accommodates the work of early AIDS mourners in important ways, especially in the insistence that death is ever present, that death is somehow always impending, and that survivors can confront all this death in the face of shame and stigma in eloquent ways that also often imply a fierce political sensibility and a longing for justice.[40]

In the face of compounded and compounding loss, grief is interminable. In Woubshet's careful study, the elegy shifts in form and function from a simple lyrical lamentation for the dead, the already gone, to "a compounded poetics of loss," wherein the mournful expressivity of the elegy registers the anticipated loss of one's own life as well. "AIDS elegies," he states succinctly, "are poems about being left behind, but they are also poems about leaving."[41]

The poem "Heavy Breathing" that appears in the collection of poems and essays *Ceremonies: Prose and Poetry* assumes an elegiac function as it documents black queer life at the end of the twentieth century. Fragmented and flowing, "Heavy Breathing" is nearly twenty pages long. The poem's broken lines reference transatlantic slavery, racialized sexual economies and violences, black suffering during the Reagan era, the sweet fervor of a drag ball, black political aspirations for bourgeois normativity, the afterglow of orgasm, and the poet's own impending death. In this poem African American life traverses four hundred years of modernity to conclude as a mere artifact for brief survey in a natural history museum. "Heavy Breathing" opens with a bus ride that traverses and entwines the post–civil rights urban landscape of Washington, DC, with the history of racial slavery and inadequate democratic achievement for African Americans after its formal abolition:[42]

> At the end of heavy breathing,
> at the beginning of grief and terror, on the X2, the bus I call a slave
>   ship. The majority of its riders Black. Pressed to journey to
>   Northeast, into voodoo ghettos
> festering on the knuckles
> of the negro dream.[43]

The stanza opens significantly the end of heavy breathing, at the passage out of life, with a reference to the affective and experiential horrors of the Middle Passage. The X2 bus is reminiscent of the slave ship despite heading northeast—that is, to the imagined site of freedom for the enslaved. Notably, the bus route begins and ends at the White House, the domestic symbol of the democratic nation. Known for the poverty of its majority-black passengers and its high incidents of violent crime, the X2 bus itself instantiates *and* transports black passengers to the place of failed freedom dreams. Later stanzas refer to the dangers of the crowded X2 bus, mainly the verbal harassment and violent sexual assault of black women and girls along the route. Instead of symbolizing socioeconomic, political, and technological improvement for black people, the X2 bus marks the persistence of (explicitly gendered and sexualized) social malaise in updated and reconfigured forms.

Setting aside the historical narrative of racial suffering, Hemphill deploys the Black Ecstatic as an affective and poetic mode to seek and celebrate the disastrous life that is. Despite its catalog of horrors, in other words, the poem refuses notions of historicity *and* futurity, as it peruses the broken cityscapes of vulnerable black life over the course of a single night seeking "Giovanni's Room in this bathhouse" and "the place where good feeling awaits me/self-destruction in my hand."[44] The invocation of James Baldwin's 1956 novel *Giovanni's Room* places Hemphill's poem within a tradition of black queer life writing. A seemingly steady voice, which might be attributed to the poet himself, describes overlapping scenes of destruction and celebration. At once despairing and euphoric, the speaker

> celebrate[s] [his] natural tendencies,
> photosynthesis, erotic customs.
> . . . .
> allow[s] [him]self to dream of roses
> though [he] know[s]
> the bloody war continues.[45]

The speaker savors, rather than refutes, the embodied pleasures that led to his fatal AIDS infection. He imagines the afterlife of death by figuring himself as the flowers that stem from and ornament graves. Nonetheless, by entwining erotic pleasures with the process by which plants convert light to energy, into fuel for activity, the poet also registers the current, defiant fight for his life.

> At the end of heavy breathing
> the funerals of my brothers
> force me to wear
> this scratchy black suit
> I should be seeding their graves.[46]

As he grieves the loss of beloved men, the poem's speaker contends with the multiplicity of abbreviated black (queer) male lives. His reference to seeding the graves of fallen lovers and comrades anticipates the speaker's own death; in time his own body will fill a grave. His vision of communal expansion is at once self-loving/pleasuring and brotherly.[47] Through the trope of organic continuity, the seed (seropositive semen) is depicted as both the contaminating agent of death and as the regenerative agent of an alternate mode of belonging—the bind that binds a community of queer black men who die violently and prematurely of disease.

An irreverent, ecstatic tone punctuates the speaker's lament. As a largely autobiographical poem, "Heavy Breathing" is an unbearably close text, as it exposes the insides of a beautiful gay black man, who is falling literally and figuratively apart:

kneeling over a fucking toilet
splattering my insides
in a stinking, shit-stained bowl
I reduce loneliness to cheap green rum,
spicy chicken, glittering vomit.
I go to the place
where danger awaits me.[48]

Sex and decay commingle in the poem, as its loose organization keeps time with the recurring phrase "at the end of heavy breathing," to mark these central themes. The poem is on a journey. Even as it grapples with common, predictable death in the early era of AIDS and crack, the poem, like its speaker, has feet. It rides on buses, steps into alleyways, cruises for sex, club-hops, surveys what is left to be seen, accumulates remembrances. In her brilliant study *Raising the Dead*, Sharon Holland poses two critical questions: "If we were in the position of the subject denied the status of the living, how would we illustrate this social condition? . . . When 'living' is something to be *achieved* and not *experienced* and figurative and literal death are very much a part of the social landscape, do people of color gain a sense of empowerment?"[49] Experimenting in verse to rework the dimensions and the demands of black queer autobiography, "Heavy Breathing" wrenches apart life, language, and love to render each a case study. The poem thereby proffers a tentative answer to Holland's questions. "I continue to awaken/shell-shocked, wondering/where I come from," the voice in the poem confesses.[50] These lines convey the exhaustion of daily life under the quotidian subjugations of racism and homophobia. Nonetheless, by returning to each day in pain *but curious*, the speaker offers a model and a methodology for subjects whose lives hover perpetually at the threshold of death. "I'm insatiable," the speaker declares:

the vampire in the garden, demented
by the blood of a succulent cock
I prowl in scant sheaths of latex.

I harbor no shame.
I solicit no pity.[51]

The speaker insists on the life he has been granted on the terms afforded for the duration of breaths allotted. His ecstasy propels him. We find the beginnings of an answer to Holland's query in the questions the poem itself asks: "Why is some destruction so beautiful?" and "*Do you think I could walk pleasantly / and well-suited toward annihilation?*"[52] The speaker in the poem is fully aware of the toll that life takes on the living, especially for the black, the queer. Almost always the result is to contract, to squelch the inner life, to reach for something different, to surrender some of the current vitality. As, again, the poem is organized around recurring pictures and phrases that demarcate new and last life, the poem records the final disordered observations of a dying man who has already survived. I do not refer here to an embodied survival, of course, but to a transcendent, ecstatic one. In the speaker's repetition of his expiration, his dying again and again, he endures. Immersed in an ever-expanding periphery, the poem thus offers a specter of what might be, an invocation of the possible. As the poem spans centuries over a single night, it contains the past, the future, and all of their interlocking injuries and possibilities in a single bounded eternity.[53] A powerful exemplar of the Black Ecstatic, "Heavy Breathing" conjures in verse the African American queer beyond, where what may be found by looking closely and closer still are inarticulable emancipatory possibilities, the barest repair, and exuberant joy in the continuing, catastrophic present.

To conclude, Lauren Berlant refers to eroticized and politicized attachments, those desired objects and outcomes that simultaneously enable and impair subjects and collectivities "fantasies that fray."[54] Her list of fraying fantasies includes "upward mobility, job security, political and social equality, and lively durable intimacy."[55] As longings that sustain *and* devitalize those bound by their appeal, fantasies that fray orient persons and populations toward life even as they usher them toward death. In a different disturbance of desire, Sharon Holland critiques the reservoir of good that putatively resides in the queer, whether person, practice, project, or politic. She disrupts the fantasy, prevalent in both activism and academia, that erotic lives, or queer practices, constitute forms of privatized subversion. She suggests, alternately, that, rather than being sites of autonomy and equivalency, the enactments of preference and pleasure that we regard as evidence and entitlement of individuated personhood are sometimes the reservoirs of racist practice.[56] The will to consume, destroy, exploit, or topple an Other, Holland reminds us, originates in desire. Desire is not intrinsically ethical or political, but it may be made so via affective transfer, social transformation, and insurgent expressive practice.

In different ways, Berlant and Holland unsettle normative notions of the good, whether inherent in our selves or in the ambition of our erotic or political will. If the longing for social equality within existing political frameworks, for example, wastes precious psychic and social resources, as Berlant suggests, even as it names the reformed world that we seek, then with what choices are we left? If our defiant visibility unwittingly diminishes our security within a lethal carceral and hypersurveillance state, then how and to whom do we say our names? The lessons of the Black Ecstatic, as taught by such practitioners as Tarell Alvin McCraney, Barry Jenkins, and Essex Hemphill, are to allow woundedness, to develop an appetite for terror, to hold on to others, to outgrow and outdo catastrophe—in order to locate the ecstasy that inevitably, if surprisingly, attends its moment and infuses its aftermath. For it is in the intersection, the churning overlap, of catastrophe and ecstasy that we may encounter a perilous and queer black freedom.

EPILOGUE

ON SUSTENANCE AND SUTURE

Thought emerges from the ruins, as the ruins.
—JUDITH BUTLER

It is commonly believed and frequently pronounced that writing the introduction to a monograph is simultaneously the most important and the most challenging part of its production. How does an academic writer account for the entire project, its central inquiry, and the constitutive elements of its argument in a guided opening? The claims of the various chapters must somehow coalesce in overarching propositions that come first, and that provide a mere sketch or map of what is to follow. It is only through constant returns to and revisions of those overarching propositions that the introduction is able to capture accurately and efficaciously the analyses that unfold within the subsequent pages of the monograph. This is common knowledge, or common wisdom, to which I generally assent. Nonetheless, for me, for *Millennial Style*, the bigger challenge is how to end it. And this has less to do with the labor of monographic scholarly production than with the state of the world into which this book emerges.

Although my primary objective throughout this study has been to identify and to recover the political undercurrents and aspirations of avant-gardist black expressive culture of recent decades, my guiding preoccupation has been with time: the recursive temporality of racial degradation and dispossession, the never-ending cycle of black political achievement and white supremacist backlash and the ensuing retrenchment, the continuing catastrophe that defines black existence in modernity. These things, this fundamental problem with time and with its movement for black subjects, belie the very notion of progress and what progress might mean for black people: our individual life spans, the promises of political inclusion and citizenship, our liberation struggles and their achievements (historic and forthcoming), our planetary existence. And, so, I began this study with a conception of time tethered to ruin. I began with ruin not because of political resignation or depression but because I believe—or understand, rather—that ruin characterizes the general state of black life: in and since the Middle Passage, in and since racial slavery. In ruin, (some form of) annihilation has already occurred. The future no longer holds the promise of betterment. On the horizon is only further crisis and harm. The devastations of disaster are everywhere evident. And these devastations must be borne because the only life on offer is life within the wreck(age).

Still, it is hard to face that in the years since first putting the first word on-screen to begin what would become *Millennial Style*, the world has experienced a global pandemic and has lost millions of lives to it. A coup was attempted in the United States to prevent the legal transfer of presidential power. Given that changes in presidential leadership have not generally entailed substantial improvement in the lives of disenfranchised, impoverished, overpoliced, imminently killable black and brown subjects, it is hard to understand the exact point of the coup. Nonetheless, its occurrence reveals something about the feverish pitch of white supremacist sentiment and political doggedness in the current moment. Rabid bias, incivility, and hatred have become normalized in popular and political discourse and are disseminated widely in everyday social encounters and virally across media. *Roe v. Wade* has been overturned. Social services for the impoverished and dispossessed continue to contract to levels heretofore unseen and unimaginable, even with the austerity and economization of human life under neoliberalism. Gun purchase and possession are almost completely deregulated, even as gun violence saturates the cultural and social landscape and has become a leading cause of death for children in the United States. Criminal justice reform and the notable conviction of murderous police and white vigilantes have done little to curb the mass warehousing and mass killing of black people by state agents. Beginning with the rise of Trumpism as a brand of brash, white supremacist, hypermasculinist, anti-intellectual, nativist, and neofascist governance in the United States and now living in the legacy of it, just about everyone I know has been reduced at one time or another to utter speechlessness in trying to account for the world as it is now. Rather than try to find the words—for which, frankly, there are none—to characterize the never-ending apocalypse, a better use of time and intellection, might be to explain how we black people endure it: with unimaginable effort, rigorous study, glorious style, relentless innovation, and sometimes (just sometimes) with joy.

In the simplest terms, *Millennial Style* is a project that iterates and theorizes the black avant-garde as an aesthetic repudiation of spectacularity—in its record of ruin *and* promise of progress—in twenty-first-century African diasporic expressive culture. My central query draws on two realizations: (1) the ubiquitous presence of blackness—black people, black vernaculars, black arts, black misery, black gesture, black style, black luminescence, black death—informs, authenticates, and enlivens every aspect of late capitalist commodity, media, carceral, and political culture in the US and beyond; and, (2) rather than read the skepticism or eschewal of realist representation in black literary and visual culture of high experiment as a flight from politics, it is necessary to develop nuanced and sophisticated analytical grammars capable of discerning their societal critique and advancing their ethical and political visions. This book has aimed to do precisely that.

By conceptualizing four distinct aesthetic modalities, I provide portable, utilizable hermeneutics for analyzing contemporary experimental black expressive forms and texts. I focus specifically on these aesthetic modes for inquiry and theory due to their unique capacity to signify and operate multiply—as innovative expressive techniques, affective resonances, and radical, if subtle, political interventions. Via regenerative art techniques such as substitution, collage, distortion, and inversion, *Black Grotesquerie* renders the boundary between black living and black dying porous and negotiable; it shifts the concern of black life from politics and performances of survival to gestures and technologies of continuance (of keeping on) by textualizing grotesquerie as a means of accepting catastrophe as the context for black being, of living on in outmoded shapes, and of recycling wreckage into sustenance. *Black Cacophony* is the enraged, despairing, lust-filled, deranged, nonmelodic sounding-off of black pain and black want in African diasporic literature, a tactic of textual representation that exposes both the insufficiency and superfluity of language for capturing exploited or discarded black life while insisting, in its sentient soundings, that such life still matters. *Black Hollows/ Hollowed Blackness* conveys the ubiquitous experiences of pursuit, capture, and containment for black subjects alongside the emotional strain of hollowness or hollowing out; in black expressive texts, the configuration of *Black Hollows* advance a black abolitionist aesthetic that alters liberationist ideologies of fugitivity by reimagining its primary architecture and reconfiguring it from the outward and external outdoors to the internal and interior hollow. Across literary and cinematic platforms, the *Black Ecstatic* reveals willful exuberance to be the affective disposition and relational ethic that enables black life and liberation in the midst of ongoing terror, crisis, and loss; it is a queer expressive modality that aestheticizes black mystery, and that synthesizes fleeting moments of black communion into an exhilarating eternality.

Managing crises as frequent and recurrent as each new day, recycling wreckage into sustenance, keeping on when there is nothing left, making last what has already been ruined—these are black modes of being. And we do this. Since they arrived, since they built forts along the shoreline, since some of us helped with the chaining and packing of our people into the bottoms of the ships, since the Middle Passage and the dispersal, since *we* arrived. We do this. Black artmakers are the ones who map and language how, even when how they show and tell defies understanding, even when they innovate modes of signifying that do not reproduce the violence of the happening. This is the black avant-garde.

At the heart of my conceptualization of ruin and of the black avant-gardist aesthetics that reckon with it is a wide-ranging, if granular, investigation into the modalities of survival and persistence, epistemologies of emergence and immanence, praxes of rupture and critique, maneuvers of sustenance and suture among black subjects enduring disasters without end. The primary offering of this book, then, is the assembly and analysis of a new millennial archive of African diasporic cultural production that reckons truly with the continuities and intricacies of political terror and that commit radically, if subtly and nonspectacularly, to an improved world for the subordinated, the exhausted, the neglected, the abandoned, the annihilated, the black. My heartfelt and deeply committed aims in writing this book and of engaging with the aesthetic objects that traverse its pages are to theorize systems and semantics of black endurance and to promote reparative (social, ethical, relational, ecological, political) infrastructures amid the ruin of our times—to quell the ruin of our lives.

ACKNOWLEDGMENTS

This book was written across three US presidencies—or, perhaps more precisely, the ideas that have culminated in this book began during the latter part of Barack Obama's second term in office, and I wrote and revised, revised and wrote, across the two presidencies that followed his. I share this information to allude to the timeline for incubating and producing a second book as an associate professor who changed institutional affiliations. I share this also to indicate the significance of political occurrence for framing and altering black cultural practice as well as the transformations in critical discourses evolved in commensurate study of it. Most relevant to my disclosure is the challenge of adequately accounting for and acknowledging all of those people, events, institutional sites, communitarian structures that allowed this book—written in and through such profound change and such profound staying-the-same—to be completed, to end up here as study, as meditation, as offering, as promise (from me to you).

I owe profound gratitude to Phillip Brian Harper, whose graduate course Problems in Representations of Blackness and whose book *Abstractionist Aesthetics: Artistic Form and Social Critique in African American Culture* first alerted me to the political undercurrents of experimental black expressive practice. Instead of viewing black abstractionist cultural production as a flight from social concern and political engagement, Harper brilliantly shifted the focus of black cultural studies to form and to black aesthetic experiments as sites of political imagination and potential sociopolitical remediation. His courageous, visionary scholarship inspires this study. My other primary teacher, whose classroom I have never entered but whose thought is the ongoing occasion and condition of possibility for my own, is Hortense

Spillers. To her I owe deep gratitude for touchstone moments in my career when a simple, if metaphorical, nod from her was permission to continue in a chosen direction. Guiding my paths of inquiry and indelibly marking them throughout this book is her field-defining scholarship on black genders, black cultures, black literatures.

For being my long-standing models of academic rigor, professional poise, interminable grace, I am indebted always to Elizabeth McHenry and Joycelyn Moody. For genuine friendship and the smartest conversations, I thank long-term besties and favorites Asha Tall, Megan Finch, beluvid ola-jendai, C. Riley Snorton, Rich Blint. The analyses developed throughout this book have benefited from astute, dedicated interlocuters, who have doubled as colleagues and friends at Brandeis University and Brown University: Faith Smith, Chad Williams, David Sherman, Ulka Anjaria, Tom King, Jasmine Johnson, Carina Ray, Paul Morrison, John Burt, John Plotz, Salah Hassan, Kevin Quashie, Matt Guterl, Leticia Alvarado, Patrick Sylvain, Timothy Bewes, Elena Shih, Kiri Miller, Wendy Lee, Alexander Weheliye, Yannis Hamilakis, Tricia Rose, Vazira Zamindar, Rolland Murray, Daniel Kim, Richard Rambuss, Ralph Rodriguez, Ariella Aïsha Azoulay, Emily Owens, Leela Gandhi, Amanda Anderson, Dixa Ramirez-D'Oleo, Olukunle George. Deep thinking and cherished conversations with scholars and friends across institutions and disciplines have refined my thought and strengthened this book immeasurably. For this, I thank Shoniqua Roach, Riché Richardson, Sandy Alexandre, Kimberly Juanita Brown, La Marr Jurelle Bruce, Samantha Pinto, Simone Browne, Jasper Verlinden, Shanté Paradigm Smalls, Ramzi Fawaz, Peter Lurie, Gershun Avilez, Dagmawi Woubshet, Yogita Goyal, LaMonda Stallings, Amber Musser, Florian Seidlmeier. It was my great fortune to work with three amazing research assistants in the English Department at Brown, whose meticulous research and care with the manuscript enabled it to emerge: Devon Clifton, Juan Gallardo, Tara Holman, thank you so very much!

Ken Wissoker saw what this book could be and believed in it before I did, and he patiently awaited its completion through the unpredictability and difficulty of pandemic times. I am convinced that Ken is the simply the best editor ever, a brilliant visionary who has both supported the careers of (variously minoritized) scholars and helped to shape fields of inquiry. I offer additional heartfelt thanks to the staff at Duke University Press for bringing this book into the world. The anonymous readers of the manuscript helped it to become what it needed to be. I am forever indebted to them. I am deeply grateful to all of the folks who invited me, joined, with me, and facilitated my participation in lectures, conferences, and symposia over the years in which work from this book was shared and from which it has been developed.

My family is my most profound treasure. I offer profound gratitude to my thirteen siblings, my beloved cothinkers and cotravelers in life. How we love and shield and hold one another each day has taught me what it is be in community, what it is to be people truly together. I miss my father, Mujahid, desperately still. My mother, my Umi, Inshirah, is my first and truest model of what it is to be human, to be Muslim, to be woman, to be person. Words inevitably fail to convey the love and awe and deep humility and hope she inspires in me. Finally, to Isa and Kamilah, my ones, around whom daily life is organized and to whom this book is dedicated: I thank you for arriving and for defining my life purpose at the vastly different times of your arrivals. Your very beingness—and the mind-blowing beauty at the heart of it—is what compels me to imagine and to seek constantly conditions of inhabitability in and of this world you have inherited.

For anyone who was there whom I have failed to mention here, please forgive me. And please know that you, too, have my sincerest gratitude.

NOTES

INTRODUCTION. TOWARD A RADICAL THEORY OF THE BLACK AVANT-GARDE

Epigraphs: Da Silva, "Hacking the Subject," 22; McKittrick, "Mathematics, Black Life," 17; Hartman, *Wayward Lives, Beautiful Experiments*, xiv.

1 Jones, *Prelude to Bruise*, 78.

2 Jones, *Prelude to Bruise*, 78.

3 Jones, *Prelude to Bruise*, 82.

4 For masterful studies that capture the disasters of the Middle Passage and embodied black slavery, please see Smallwood, *Saltwater Slavery*; Hartman, *Scenes of Subjection*; Patterson, *Slavery and Social Death*; Jones, *Birthright Citizens*; Johnson, *Soul by Soul*; and Fuentes, *Dispossessed Lives*.

5 I am thinking here with Judith Butler. In her brief essay "After Loss, What Then?," Butler contemplates "the strange fecundity of that wreckage." Wreckage refers here to what remains after profound loss: genocidal loss, the loss of dispossession, the loss of colonial subjection, the loss of conditions for livability. She suggests that these losses give rise not only to new modalities of political subjectification and collective agency but also to the formation of collectivities bound by memorializing and surviving these profound losses (in Eng and Kazanjian, *Loss*, 469).

6 My brief sketch of the police murder of Michael Brown and the movement for black lives does not convey their deep meanings and impacts. I recall them here briefly in order to explain the moment and meditation that inspired this book. For a thoughtful (historical, political, and ideological) treatment, see Keeanga-Yamahtta Taylor, *From #blacklivesmatter to Black Liberation*.

7 It is neither hyperbolic nor melodramatic to recall that for centuries millions of African Americans were held in generational racial slavery. Thus, while recognizing that sustainable black liberation has not been achieved, what I allude to here are the various freedom movements that have been successful in terms legislation and

political inclusion, most specifically the abolitionist and civil rights movement. Despite formal liberation from enslavement and its aftermath, freedom has never materialized for the overwhelming majority of black people.

8 Morrison, *Source of Self-Regard*, ix.

9 Harper, *Abstractionist Aesthetics*.

10 There are many excellent studies of persistence and permutations of antiblack racism, anti-immigrant hysteria, and xenophobia in the decades after the legislative successes of the civil rights movement, including Bonilla-da Silva, *Racism without Racists*; Anderson, *White Rage*; Kendi, *Stamped from the Beginning*; Alexander, *New Jim Crow*; and Roberts, *Fatal Invention*.

11 McKittrick, "Mathematics, Black Life," 17.

12 McKittrick, "Mathematics, Black Life," 17.

13 McKittrick, "Mathematics, Black Life," 17.

14 Authoritative texts that theorize the avant-garde, and that inform my understanding and reconceptualization of it, include Bürger, *Theory of the Avant-Garde*; Adorno, *Aesthetic Theory*; and Foster, *Return of the Real*.

15 Foster, *Return of the Real*, 4.

16 My thinking about the deleterious impacts of a turn to multicultural discourse and the institutionalization of multiculturalism as the cultural ideal and political agenda in the post–civil rights moment is informed by the general abandonment of commitment to redistributive socioeconomic and political justice. I think it is important to note that this problematic political redirection was enabled and reflected by the increase of black politicians in local, state, and federal governance; it was also occasioned by a reshaping of the priorities of liberal education and the renovation of the global image of the United States during the Cold War era. For more in-depth treatment, see, in particular, Silva's monumental *Toward a Global Idea of Race*; and Melamed's incomparable *Represent and Destroy*.

17 For more on this point, please see the following highly influential books: Cohen, *Boundaries of Blackness*; Mbembe, *Necropolitics*; and Duggan, *Twilight of Equality*.

18 Jones, "Infinite Ache."

19 Allen, *There Is a Disco Ball*, xv.

20 Best, *None Like Us*, 37.

21 While not in complete agreement with Best or Brown, I, nevertheless, share their critique of political mobilization organized around narratives of racial harm that presume that such harm can be suitably quantified and narrativized in a complaint for political remedy, which typically comes in the form of legislative amendment. The mode of political achievement takes for granted that there are suitable discursive frames, whether literary or legalistic, that can understand devastating, incomprehensible racial crimes and that proposed remedies are necessarily forthcoming, effective, or enduring. For a thorough exposition of her points, see Brown, *States of Injury*.

22 Best, *None Like Us*, 2.

23 Best, *None Like Us*, 10.

24 Keeling, *Queer Time, Black Futures*, 17.

25 Keeling, *Queer Time, Black Futures*, 18–19.
26 Sullivan, *Poetics of Difference*, 183.
27 Sullivan, *Poetics of Difference*, 38.
28 Nyong'o, *Afro-Fabulations*, 153.
29 Nyong'o, *Afro-Fabulations*, 165.
30 Jones, *Prelude to Bruise*, 68.
31 I am thinking here with other theorists of black subjectification under conditions of colonial subjections and political annihilation, including Franz Fanon, Silvia Wynter, Jared Sexton, and Alexander Weheliye. All theorize the excision of the black from the category of the human and the black as the figure that defines the properties of the human via the inapplicability and nullification of those properties.
32 I refer now to recent studies of African American literature and culture that reconsider long-standing critical presumptions about the relationship between black cultural production and sociopolitical intervention. Like this book, these studies register skepticism about the prevailing belief that mimetic realism best conveys black experience and that it necessarily promotes and produces sociopolitical repair.
33 Reed, *Freedom Time*; Crawford, *Black Post-Blackness*, Best, *None Like Us*; Keeling, *Queer Times, Black Futures*; and Harper, *Abstractionist Aesthetics* all explore the interrelatedness of black expressive form and African American political life.
34 Díaz, *Brief Wondrous Life*, 1; Morrison, *Beloved*, 181.
35 Bloch, "Discussing Expressionism," 22.
36 Da Silva, *Toward a Global Idea of Race*, xxxv.
37 Da Silva, "Hacking the Subject," 21.
38 Da Silva, "Hacking the Subject," 27.

CHAPTER 1. BLACK GROTESQUERIE

Epigraphs: Muñoz, *Disidentifications*, 66; Bakhtin, *Rabelais and His World*, 21; Wilderson, *Red, White and Black*, 99.

1 Blackman, *Tradition*, 3.
2 By alluding to the political case on behalf of and investment in black life, I am suggesting that the general orientation and aspiration of black political movements (historically and into the present) are equitable quality of life, sustainable socioeconomic conditions, and improved life chances for black people. The essential harm of antiblackness—as decried in black movements—is the disparate vulnerability of black people to premature death. This notably crosses institutions, industries, economic status, and time periods. Diminished, abbreviated life is the fatal consequence of antiblackness.
3 I refer to and expand the colloquialism *living on* to invoke, first, the way that the dead continue into the present, usually in memory but also in the process of (physiological) change after death. Second, I refer to surviving in the face of disastrous circumstances and impossible odds.
4 Central to my theory of Black Grotesquerie is an investigation into the ongoing

relationship between social abjection and literary abstraction. I am guided in this intellectual undertaking by Phillip Brian Harper's *Abstractionist Aesthetics: Artistic Form and Social Critique in African American Culture.* Insisting on abstractionism's "potential for engendering social critique," Harper makes a compelling case for reconsidering evaluative standards in black expressive culture that regard realism as epitomizing racially affirmative political commitment (179).

5 Bakhtin, *Rabelais and His World*, 21.

6 Bakhtin, *Rabelais and His World*, 10.

7 Bakhtin, *Rabelais and His World*, 10.

8 Hartman, "Venus in Two Acts," 6.

9 Hartman, "Venus in Two Acts," 12.

10 This is the phrase used by Frank B. Wilderson III in his radio interview with Jared Ball, Todd Steven Burroughs, and Dr. Hate, hosts of IMIXWHATILIKE, titled "We're Trying to Destroy the World" (16–17).

11 I am very grateful to my friend and Brandeis colleague David Sherman for helping me to think through this point, to name this practice.

12 For innovative and nuanced studies on the intersection of race and temporality, see Anthony Reed's *Freedom Time*, particularly chapter 3, "Between Now and Yet: Postlyric Poetry and the Time of Expression"; and the introduction to Michelle Wright's *The Physics of Blackness.* Both texts take as central themes how notions of race and of racial uplift depend on notions of time, of history, and promised futurity.

13 Sexton, "Social Life of Social Death," 6.

14 Crenshaw, "Du Bois Lecture."

15 Polls conducted around the time of Barack Obama's election that asked respondents to consider its historical meanings indicate the belief that racial attitudes have become more progressive and structural racism has essentially disappeared in the United States.

16 Colin Dayan, "With Law," 630.

17 Rodriguez, *Forced Passages*, 6.

18 For more on the racialized history of welfare and the impacts of welfare reform on black families since the 1990s, see chapter 4 of my *Against the Closet.*

19 Ruth Wilson Gilmore in *Golden Gulag* and Dylan Rodriguez in *Forced Passages* have informed my thinking about mass incarceration and the abrogation of black citizenship initially in the postslavery and now in the post–civil rights era.

20 Colin Dayan decries Obama's perpetuation of legally sanctioned modes of mass confinement and, specifically, his legitimation of extralegal imprisonment and targeted, slow death. By emphasizing Obama's role in the expansion of the carceral industry, along with its innovative standards of long-term, extrajudicial confinement, Dayan highlights the failure of Obama's presidency to actualize African American political hopes for racial equality in the current century. Rather than effectuating long-awaited socioeconomic and political improvement in the lives of racially marked, marginalized populations, Obama is implicated in the very systems of oppression that disproportionately harm them.

21 Childs, *Slaves of the State*, 275.

22 Rodriguez, *Forced Passages*, 11.

23 This is general comment on carceral capitalism. For an excellent study of this, see Jackie Wang's *Carceral Capitalism*.

24 The grotesque is strongly correlated to abjection through a shared conceptual and rhetorical emphasis on bodily deformity and porosity. Frantz Fanon describes the frequent, mundane experiences of abjection primarily in terms of corporeal demarcation; "consciousness of the body is solely a negating activity" he writes (110). Inhabiting the debased position of the black, Fanon describes racialized abjection primarily as trauma, fragmentation, and the constant threat of psychic dissolution and bodily demise: "I subjected myself to an objective examination, I discovered my blackness, my ethnic characteristics; and I was battered down by tom-toms, cannibalism, intellectual deficiency, fetichism, racial defects, slave ships, and above all else: 'sho' good eatin'. . . . What else could it be for me but an amputation, an excision, a hemorrhage that spattered my whole body with black blood?" (112). Although Fanon does not relinquish entirely his claim to a (semi)autonomous subjectivity that can think and act on its own behalf, his activities reveal nonetheless the embodied violences of racialized abjection. The leaky substances that indicate for Fanon psychic compromise are those with which abject bodies are always affiliated—pus, sweat, blood, excrement, vomit.

25 Following and extending Orlando Patterson's seminal work on social death, Lisa Marie Cacho studies social death as a primary feature of racialization and criminalization. See Cacho, *Social Death*; and Dayan, *Law Is a White Dog*.

26 Hartman, "Belly of the World," 168.

27 Jackson, *Becoming Human*, 167.

28 Stoler, *Duress*, 7.

29 Stoler, *Duress*, 7.

30 Barber and Naimou, "Between Disgust and Regeneration," 340.

31 Hernandez, "Ambivalent Grotesque," 433.

32 For nuanced and detailed explication of this point, see da Silva, "Hacking the Subject."

33 Wynter, "Unsettling the Coloniality of Being," 257–337.

34 Spillers, "Mama's Baby, Papa's Maybe," 67.

35 For an excellent excursus on black feminist theories of the human, see Alexander Weheliye's masterful account of Hortense Spillers's and Sylvia Wynter's work in the introduction to *Habeas Viscus*.

36 Ann Stoler powerfully theorizes resurgencies in her studies of imperial duress.

37 A recent and poignant study on Emmett Till's murder and its powerful influence on the civil rights movement may be found in Anderson, *Emmett Till*.

38 Moten, "Black Mo'nin," 63–64.

39 In her book *In the Wake: On Blackness and Being*, Christina Sharpe offers one of the most incisive and compelling investigations of the similar conditions of oceanic travel endured by African and Muslim refugees in the present and those endured by captives Africans during the Middle Passage. Her analysis attends to the cramped containment, the inadequate sustenance, the constancy of violence and demise.

40 Bakhtin, *Rabelais and His World*, 8.

41 Edwards and Grauland, *Grotesque*, 123.

42 Bakhtin, *Rabelais and His World*, 26.

43 Bakhtin, *Rabelais and His World*, 378.

44 Hortense Spillers describes the racialization of the black by and in enslavement as a simultaneous process of ungendering. This conception of the ungendering of the black is tied to her account of the flesh and its distinction from the body—the primary possession of the citizen-subject. See "Mama's Baby, Papa's Maybe."

45 Blackman, *Tradition*, 192.

46 For a detailed account of racial science in the development of sexual epistemologies, including the figuring of black women's bodies in that work, see my introduction to *Against the Closet*.

47 "The difficulty a mother has in acknowledging (or being acknowledged by) the symbolic realm—in other words, the problem she has with the phallus that her father or her husband stands for—is not such as to help the future subject leave the natural mansion. The child can serve its mother as token of her own authentication; there is, however, hardly any reason for her to serve as go-between for it to become autonomous and authentic in its turn. In such close combat, the symbolic light that a third party, eventually the father, can contribute helps the future subject, the more so if it happens to be endowed with a robust supply of drive energy, in pursuing a reluctant struggle against what, having been the mother, will turn into an abject." Kristeva, *Powers of Horror*, 13.

48 Blackman, *Tradition*, 196–97.

49 Blackman, *Tradition*, 99.

50 Blackman, *Tradition*, 102.

51 Blackman, *Tradition*, 269.

52 Blackman, *Tradition*, 28.

53 Blackman, *Tradition*, 271.

54 Wilderson, *Red, White and Black*, 55.

CHAPTER 2. HOLLOWED BLACKNESS

Epigraphs: Holland, *Raising the Dead: Readings of Death and (Black) Subjectivity*, 18; Tariq, *Heed the Hollow: Poems*.

1 Monet, *My Mother Was a Freedom Fighter*, 97–98.

2 Monet, *My Mother Was a Freedom Fighter*, 97–98.

3 Jared Sexton's "People-of-Color-Blindness: Notes on the Afterlife of Slavery" shifts the discourse of bare life from the figure of Agamben's refugee to the figure of Hartman's enslaved black female. Though Sexton doesn't pay much attention to the "affective range" and "emotive drains" of barely living, this concern comes up in Alexander Weheliye's revisions of Agamben in *Habeas Viscus*.

4 Kevin Quashie writes in *Sovereignty of Quiet: Beyond Resistance in Black Culture* that "quiet is the subjectivity that permits the vagary of humanity and that pushes against social identity and its narrow corners. Quiet is desire, and vulnerability; it

is disarray, the willingness to give up the seduction of saying your name clearly and singularly, as a stay against the world. Quiet is related to the names you call yourself, the ones that cannot be spelled or fully pronounced. Quiet is uncertain and it is sure; trembling and arrogant. Quiet is faith in that it can embrace what there is little evidence of. Quiet can exist without horizon, and it has no consecutive. Quiet is like the moon, rarely showing its full wondrous sphere and instead offering slivers of its potent, tide-shifting self" (134).

5 See Fred Moten and Saidiya Hartman in conversation at Duke University as part of Black Outdoors series. At approximately twenty-nine minutes, Hartman talks about the fugitive hiding in a hollowed out tree. YouTube video, 2:04:03, October 5, 2016, https://www.youtube.com/watch?v=t_tUZ6dybrc&t=1743s.

6 In his magnificent book *How to Go Mad without Losing Your Mind: Madness and Black Radical Creativity*, La Marr Jurelle Bruce ponders Samuel Cartwright's 1851 coinage of the term *drapetomania* as a form of racialized derangement that caused enslaved black people to flee. As Bruce notes, this diagnosis reflected "an antiblack antebellum insistence on conflating blackness and slaveness" (17).

7 Tariq, *Heed the Hollow*, 39.

8 Sharpe, *In the Wake*, 90.

9 For more on this point, see Saidiya Hartman's *Scenes of Subjection*; Wilderson, *Red, White, and Black*; Sharpe, *In the Wake*; and Warren, *Ontological Terror*. This is undoubtedly a partial list.

10 Whitehead, *Underground Railroad*, 152.

11 For more in-depth examinations of US railroads and the penal system, see Child, *Slaves of the State*; Blackmon, *Slavery by Another Name*; LeFlouria, *Chained in Silence*; and Haley, *No Mercy Here*.

12 McKittrick, *Demonic Grounds*, 40.

13 Whitehead, *Underground Railroad*, 223.

14 Whitehead, *Underground Railroad*, 221–22.

15 Whitehead, *Underground Railroad*, 80.

16 Whitehead, *Underground Railroad*, 223.

17 See Reid-Pharr, "At Home in America."

18 Whitehead, *Underground Railroad*, 292.

19 Monique Allewart argues in the chapter titled "Swamp Sublime: Ecology and Resistance in the American Planation Zone" of her book *Ariel's Ecology* that "instead of simply producing subjects who gained power through an abstracting print culture, the plantation zone witnessed the emergence of persons who gained agency by combining with ecological forces" occasioned by the presence of areas like swamplands (30). Drawing on William Bartram's 1791 account in *Travels* of his time in the Georgia sea islands where he records his observations of enslaved African habitation and cooperation with the ecological forces of the swamps, she asserts: "Swamps threatened colonials' efforts to separate themselves from the natural world, but it was rebellious Africans who most clearly made swamps revolutionary.... If *Travels* testifies to an ecological cycle that consumes the history and subjectivity of white men, this unpublished tract suggests that Africans will somehow

be able to use this ecology to destroy plantation societies unless state powers act first and abolish slavery" (37–41).

20 LaRoche, *Free Black Communities*, 87–88.

21 Whitehead, *Underground Railroad*, 294.

22 It is important to note that the enslaved were integrated into the sociopolitical and economic infrastructures of society but as subhuman service class/caste. The enslaved did not exist outside of the social and political landscape but, rather, lent substance and credence to the formation and operations of both by virtue of the social negation and political nullification of enslaved black people.

23 For a full explanation of "natal alienation," see Patterson, *Slavery and Social Death*. It is here that Patterson coins the term to explain the ruptures in kinship structures that racial slavery legalized and enforced to alienated the enslaved from lines of descent in terms of both ancestry and progeny.

24 Dennis Child writes in *Slaves of the State*, "Chattel slavery [is] a primordial and tenaciously undead carceral regime of Euro- American modernity—as the legal, political, architectural, and cultural linchpin of racial capitalist misogynist imprisonment in the United States as it has morphed from the slave-ship holds and barracoons of the Middle Passage, to the portable boxcar cages of early Jim Crow apartheid, to the coffin-simulating boxcar cells of today's prison—industrial complex (PIC). Indeed, when read as one overarching, cross-fertilizing, and temporally unfixed network of racial and spatial terror, the U.S. system of mass imprisonment represents a centuries-old regime of chattelized prison—industrial genocide that began well before the term PIC was ever uttered—a liberal white supremacist misogynist 'shit-stem,' as Peter Tosh might have dubbed it, that has submitted an as yet uncalculated (nor completed) number of black people and other racially and criminally stigmatized groups to collectivized natal alienation, excremental internment, (un)productive forced labor, serialized corporeal rupture, legally unredressable sexual violence, coerced performance, and manifold forms of death, ranging from the social, to the civil, to the biological" (2).

25 Whitehead, *Underground Railroad*, 295.

26 Sarah Johnson discusses the trade of specially trained attack dogs from the Caribbean to the southern United States in *The Fear of French Negroes* as a terror device used by slave catchers against subjects using the natural terrain as an emancipatory site, "insurgent slaves, maroons in revolt, and steadfast native populations resisting relocation" (35).

27 Crawford, "*Inside Turned Out* Architecture," 72.

28 Friedman, "Unsentimental Historicizing," 128.

29 Whitehead, *Underground Railroad*, 90.

30 Authoritative studies on the neo–slave narrative as a genre include Rushdy, *Neo-slave Narratives*; Diggs, Patterson, and Levy-Hussen, *Psychic Hold of Slavery*; and Keizer, *Black Subjects*.

31 See Weinstein, "Slave Narrative and Sentimental Identification," 115–34; and Shirley, *Culture of Sentiment*.

32 Crawford, "*Inside Turned Out* Architecture," 71.

33 For more on the historical phenomena of freedmen's towns, see McDavid, "When Is 'Gone' Gone?," 74–88; and Corn, *Ground on Which I Stand*. For more on maroon societies, see Alpers, "Idea of Marronage"; Roberts, *Freedom as Marronage*; and Brown, "Social Death and Political Life."
34 Whitehead, *Underground Railroad*, 256–57.
35 Whitehead, *Underground Railroad*, 303–4.
36 Quashie, *Sovereignty of Quiet*, 21.
37 Reynolds, "Alexandria Smith's First Solo Boston Show Navigates the Duality of Existence," WBUR, November 5, 2018, https://www.wbur.org/news/2018/11/05/alexandria-smith-litany-for-survival-boston.
38 Da Silva, "To Be Announced," 59.
39 Da Silva, "To Be Announced," 50.
40 hooks, "Love as the Practice of Freedom," 289–98.
41 Perry, *Vexy Thing*, 216.
42 Monet, *My Mother Was a Freedom Fighter*, 23–24.

CHAPTER 3. BLACK CACOPHONY

Epigraphs: Nichanian, "Catastrophic Mourning," 99; Glissant, *Caribbean Discourse*, 123; Keene, *Annotations*, 61.

1 Morrison, *Beloved*, 305.
2 Morrison, *Beloved*, 194.
3 Glissant, *Poetics of Relation*, 5.
4 Morrison, *Beloved*, 5.
5 Holland, *Raising the Dead*, 53.
6 See Austin, *How to Do Things with Words*. Mae G. Henderson states in "Speaking in Tongues" that "besides designating an object of affection, the term beloved occurs in matrimonial and eulogistic discourse. Both are commemorative, linguistic events: the former prefiguring the future, the latter refiguring the past" (81).
7 Diaz, *Brief and Wondrous Life*, 1.
8 Morrison, *Beloved*, 213.
9 Morrison, *Beloved*, 305.
10 In *Beloved*, Morrison writes that Ella's "puberty was spent in a house where she was shared by father and son, whom she called 'the lowest yet.' It was 'the lowest yet' who gave her a disgust for sex and against who she measured all atrocities. A killing, a kidnap, a rape—whatever, she listened and nodded. Nothing compared to 'the lowest yet" (256). Darieck Scott argues in *Extravagant Abjection* that Morrison's obscuration of scenes of spectacular violence reveals the everydayness of such egregious violence on slave plantations. He argues further: "This strategy of retreat preserves the tenderness of our sensibilities on the one hand, and on the other refuses a spectacle that might too easily portray the suffering visited on black people as a prurient and sadomasochistic entertainment" (134).
11 Henderson, "Speaking in Tongues," 74.
12 Lacan, "Mirror Stage," 75–81.

13 Glissant, *Caribbean Discourse*, 124.

14 Derrida, *Of Grammatology*.

15 See Lacan, "Excommunication," 11; Felman, "Theaters of Justice," 201–38; Hirsch, *Generation of Postmemory*; and Fink, *Lacanian Subject*.

16 This is in reference to Rancière's theories of political subjectification through reasoned dialogue.

17 Brown, "Lecture," 82.

18 Dayan, *Law Is a White Dog*.

19 Robert B. Stepto, Henry Louis Gates Jr., Houston Baker, and other architects of black literary studies make these arguments about antebellum slave narratives. Ronald Judy writes in *Disforming the American Canon*, for example, that one of the primary motivations for the production of the antebellum slave narrative was "to effect an interpolation into Western modernity's economy of signification where literacy equals Reason equals culture and civility" (71).

20 I am thinking of work by, among others, Sander Gilman, Susan Buck-Morss, George Frederickson, and, most recently, Michelle Wright.

21 See da Silva, "Toward a Black Feminist Poethics," 81–97; McKittrick, *Demonic Grounds*; Spillers, "Mama's Baby, Papa's Maybe"; and Wynter, *On Being Human as Praxis*.

22 My essay on Faulkner's *Absalom, Absalom* reads and redeems Jim Bond's howl. That analysis informs my reading of Jimmy Holiday.

23 I am thinking here of prominent scholars of African American literary studies, many of whom have developed the field by exploring and conceptualizing the slave narrative as the inaugural genre of African American literature.

24 Moten, *In the Break*, 6.

25 See Sharpe, *Monstrous Intimacies*.

26 Douglass, *Narrative of the Life*, 18.

27 Abdur-Rahman, "Strangest Freaks of Despotism," 24–50.

28 Saidiya Hartman, Meina Yates-Richard, and Fred Moten are important scholars for my thinking here. Each asserts the importance of the black maternal soundings, evoking and epitomizing of the brutalities of racial bondage, in the development of empowered, autonomous black masculinities and heteropatriarchal discourses of (juridically recognized, sociopolitically entitled, liberal) black being and advancement.

29 In his introduction to *Thoughts and Sentiments on the Evil of Slavery*, Vincent Carretta states that of the four slave narratives published in Britain in the late eighteenth century, Cugoano's was the most politically radical. Carretta bases this claim in part on Cugoano's insistence on the emancipation of all enslaved black people in Europe and throughout its colonies, rather than the mere abolition of the transatlantic slave trade. Carretta emphasizes further that the tone of Cugoano's text is confrontational and critical of both black enslavement and European imperialist conquest. The narrative appears without any authenticating document, suggesting that its antislavery arguments have not been supervised or modulated by a white editor or patron. The narrative takes the form of a political sermon and, with prophetic authority, indicts the regime of racial slavery.

30 The Redress Project, "Why History Matters," July 30, 2006, https://www.inthe medievalmiddle.com/2006/07/why-history-matters-redux-redress.html.
31 Judy, *Disforming the American Cannon*, 71–72.
32 Best and Hartman, "Fugitive Justice," 1–2.
33 Best and Hartman, "Fugitive Justice," 2.
34 Best and Hartman, "Fugitive Justice," 2.
35 Douglass, *Narrative of the Life*, 14.
36 Yates-Richard, "What Is Your Mother's Name?," 483.
37 This is contrary to Enlightenment notions of rationality as a feature of western Man.
38 Du Bois, *Souls of Black Folk, 191.*
39 Du Bois, *Souls of Black Folk*, 192.
40 Du Bois, *Souls of Black Folk*, 10.
41 Best and Hartman, "Fugitive Justice," 9.
42 Brown, "Freedom's Silences," 83.
43 Brown, "Freedom's Silences," 84.
44 Weheliye, *Habeas Viscus*, 12.
45 Moten, Fred. "Black Mo'nin,'" 65.
46 De Veaux, *Yabo*, 24–25.
47 De Veaux, *Yabo*, 26.
48 De Veaux, *Yabo*, 24–26.
49 The African baobab trees have traveled to the New World and may now be found in the Caribbean.
50 De Veaux, *Yabo*, 35.
51 De Veaux, *Yabo*, 39–40.
52 Following the prominent economist and musicologist Jacques Attali, Salomé Voegelin posits: "Seeing always happens in a meta-position, away from the seen, however close. [This] visual 'gap' nurtures the idea of certainty and the notion that we can truly understand things, give them names, and define ourselves in relation to those names as stable subjects, as identities. . . . [and this is Deleuze's account of Kant]" (*Listening to Noise and Silence*, xii).
53 Deleuze, *Difference and Repetition*, 133.
54 De Veaux, *Yabo*, 26.
55 Voegelin posits that "hearing does not offer a meta-position; there is no place where I am not simultaneous with the heard. However far its source, the sound sits in my ear. . . . Hearing involves the listener as intersubjectively constituted in perception, while producing the very thing [s]he perceives, and both, the subject and the work, thus generated concomitantly, are as transitory as each other" (*Listening to Noise and Silence*, xii).
56 Marianne Kielian-Gilbert writes that sound actualizes being "in the middle of things without being contained by them (moving between conditions and/or upper and lower limits), articulations of becoming and remembering engage aesthetic zones of asymmetrical exchange (contagion, infection) in which something of one passes into another" ("Music and Difference in Becoming," 199–226).

57 De Veaux, *Yabo*, 58.

58 Holiday, "The Black Catatonic Scream," August 20, 2020, https://www.canopy canopycanopy.com/contents/the-black-catatonic-scream.

59 Holiday, "Black Catatonic Scream."

60 Nichanian, "Catastrophic Mourning," 112.

61 Nichanian, "Catastrophic Mourning," 112.

62 I am thinking once again with La Marr Jurelle Bruce here, who carefully notes that madness contains both irrationality and rage.

63 Julia Barossa writes: "Psychoanalysis recognizes the haunting of the past within the present and is predicated on the fact, or the hope, that it can provide us with the language to speak that past, giving us 'the words to say it', the means to perceive and represent our scars, not as shameful and debilitating, but as testimonials to love and loss, the necessary price of our continued existence amongst others" ("Identity, Loss, and the Mother Tongue," 394). See also Ganteau and Onega, *Contemporary Trauma Narratives*.

64 Douglas Crimp writes in "Mourning and Militancy" that "the violence we counter is relentless, the violence of silence and omission almost as impossible to endure as the violence of unleashed hatred and outright murder. Because this violence also desecrates the memories of our dead, we rise in anger to vindicate them. For many of us, mourning *becomes* militancy" (8–9). Writing specifically rage as pervasive affect structuring and underlying the narrative in Alice Walker's *Meridian*, Jones argues, "If mourning is the call to engagement, then rage must be the response. Rage is a form of militancy that does not insist on suffering, humility, or death. . . . While grief elicits sympathy, rage implicates the interlocutor as participant in the inflicted attack or failing to protect the victim from said trauma, and, thus, is also a call to accountability. . . . While grief focuses on the dead, what is lost, rage connects the living to the dead by insisting on the value of the dead and also demanding accountability for the living, a responsibility to those who remain" ("Presenting Our Bodies," 192).

65 Holiday, "Black Catatonic Scream."

66 Holiday, "Black Catatonic Scream."

67 Holiday, "Black Catatonic Scream."

68 Therí Pickens writes: "The Black mad future is not fathomable because its present and its past are unclear. . . . [Black madness] is mutually constituted in historical terms but cannot be adequately delineated by projects that recuperate its presence or celebrate it as radical. The presence of Black madness allows for a partial unmaking of the logics that govern the linear progressive idea of time and space. Blackness and madness discomfort and confuse, particularly in intimate spaces where their cleaving is not possible" (*Black Madness*, 49).

69 Holiday, "Black Catatonic Scream."

70 Holiday and Denise, "The Sound of Getting Out," presented at the Omniaudience (Side Two), Coaxial Arts, Los Angeles, CA, May 5, 2019.

71 Nichanian, "Catastrophic Mourning," 113.

CHAPTER 4. THE BLACK ECSTATIC

Epigraphs: Muñoz, *Cruising Utopia*, 1; Butler, "Afterword," 467; Walker, *The Way Forward Is with a Broken Heart.*

1 Muñoz, *Cruising Utopia*, 1.
2 Butler, "Afterword," 467.
3 Muñoz, *Cruising Utopia*, 1.
4 Muñoz, *Cruising Utopia*, 187.
5 Muñoz, *Cruising Utopia*, 186–87.
6 Since 2015, the *Washington Post* has maintained a database that records the number of police killings in the United States. See https://www.washingtonpost.com/graphics/investigations/police-shootings-database/.
7 The persistence of the most egregious forms of racialized harm following the legislative gains of black freedom movements from emancipation through the civil rights movement has been well documented. Eduardo Bonilla-Silva's *Racism without Racists: Color-Blind Racism and the Persistence of Inequality in America*, Michelle Alexander's *The New Jim Crow: Mass Incarceration in the Era of Colorblindness*, Lisa Marie Cacho's *Social Death: Racialized Rightlessness and the Criminalization of the Unprotected*, Frank Wilderson's *Red, White, and Black: Cinema and the Structure of U.S. Antagonisms*, Colin Dayan's *The Law Is a White Dog: How Legal Rituals Make and Unmake Persons*, and Saidiya Hartman's *Lose Your Mother: A Journey along the Atlantic Slave Route* are masterful examinations of the permutations of antiblack racism in various periods of putative black advancement. They expose antiblackness as endemic to the very project of modernity, rooted in the transatlantic slave trade and ever present in newer, more abstract iterations of psychosocial and structural racism.
8 Jennifer Nash's *The Black Body in Ecstasy: Reading Race, Reading Pornography* is a book-length study on ecstasy that centers black women. Developing an alternate archive of black women's sexuality, one that pushes beyond its usual enclosures in shame, silence, and secrecy, Nash analyzes racialized pornography as an expressive mode that makes legible black women's sexual agency, energy, and joy. Significantly, in her formulation, ecstasy exceeds the corporeal pleasures of the erotic; it makes possible black women's dual experience of racial blackness as the site of deep historical wounding and of potential healing. Nash's celebration of black women's eroticism, of black women's desires and pleasures, pushes black feminist thought into the domain of black queer studies. While her investment in explicit representational and visual economies moves in a different direction from my interest here in opacity and aesthetic abstraction within black queer cultural production, her conception of ecstasy as the fraught index of relational racial pleasure is an important framework for consideration here.
9 My thinking about willfulness as a politically informed, queer way of being and as a mode of resistant action is informed by Sara Ahmed's work on willfulness. See Ahmed, *Cultural Politics of Emotion*, 12. *Willfulness* connotes not merely the deter-

mination to enact individual volition but, more importantly, to enact transformation of the status quo.

10 Aida Levy-Hussen's *How to Read African American Literature: Post-Civil Rights Fiction and the Task of Interpretation* proposes new modes of engaging in the literary interpretation of black writing after the civil rights movement. Her book expertly the limits of a particular literary approach that addresses the abstraction of state racism in the current era through fantasy returns to the antebellum era.

11 La Berge, "Rules of Abstraction," 106.

12 La Berge, "Rules of Abstraction," 96.

13 Barrett, *Racial Blackness*, 2.

14 Reed, *Freedom Time*, 207.

15 Reed, *Freedom Time*, 207.

16 brown, *Pleasure Activism*, 12.

17 Del Barco, "Growing Up Black, Gay, and Poor," NPR, October 18, 2016.

18 Del Barco, "Growing Up Black, Gay, and Poor."

19 Kafka and Brod, *Blue Octavo Notebooks*, 26.

20 For more on viral black male death and black cinema and visual culture in the 1990s, see Neale, *Looking for Leroy*; and Marriott, *On Black Men*.

21 Young, *Embodying Black Experience*, 12.

22 Young, *Embodying Black Experience*, 12.

23 Spillers, "Women and the Early Republics."

24 The question of privacy and of the politics of representational obscurity conclude my first book, *Against the Closet: Black Political Longing and the Erotics of Race*. The current essay builds on that study by analyzing politics of experiment in the black cultural expression of the putatively postracial era.

25 Dove, *Grace Notes*, 64.

26 "To insist upon a group's 'right to opacity' in sociocultural terms," writes Kara Keeling, "is to challenge the processes of commensuration built into the demand for the group to become perceptible according to the existing conceptions of the world" (*Queer Times, Black Futures*, 31). Following Keeling's compelling assertion, I would argue that this is precisely why practices of representational obscurity and obfuscation in black expressive texts are so politically promising.

27 My thinking here is informed by critical reassessments of the interrelation between queer erotics and the politics of visuality that so informs the history and political strategies of LGBTQ activism. The critique of "coming out" as a progressivist narrative of modern subjectivity and possessive individualism has been explored thoroughly in queer of color scholarship.

28 Sexton, *Black Masculinity*, 180, 181.

29 Crawley, *Black Pentecostal Breath*, 99.

30 Rankine, "Condition of Black Life," 147.

31 Berlant, "Subject of True Feeling," 53.

32 Berlant, "Subject of True Feeling," 72.

33 Berlant, "Subject of True Feeling," 53.

34 Berlant, "Subject of True Feeling," 72.

35 Berlant, "Subject of True Feeling," 62.
36 Seshadri, *HumAnimal*, 21.
37 Butler, *Undoing Gender*, 20.
38 Butler, *Undoing Gender*, 20.
39 There is not a lot of information available about Essex Hemphill's personal life outside of his published work. For an informative biography, see Duberman, *Hold Tight Gently*. Duberman manages to cull a great deal about Hemphill's life, romances, and activism by through nuanced reading of that published work.
40 Woubshet, *Calendar of Loss*, 5.
41 Woubshet, *Calendar of Loss*, 30.
42 Woubshet contends that the speaker in "Heavy Breathing" observes along the X2 bus route "not only a panorama of an American city in the '80s under siege—by government neglect, racism, violence, crack, and AIDS—but also an introspective, foreboding sense of his [the speaker's/the poet's] own upcoming death" (8) "Heavy Breathing" hails Hemphill's death as it "also articulates an inventory of loss that exceeds any finite measurement" (8).
43 Hemphill, *Ceremonies*, 6.
44 Hemphill, *Ceremonies*, 12.
45 Hemphill, *Ceremonies*, 5.
46 Hemphill, *Ceremonies*, 8.
47 Hemphill, *Ceremonies*, 12.
48 Hemphill, *Ceremonies*, 8.
49 Holland, *Raising the Dead*, 16.
50 Hemphill, *Ceremonies*, 5.
51 Hemphill, *Ceremonies*, 4.
52 Holland, *Raising the Dead*, 5.
53 Darius Bost has produced an astute and compelling analysis of Essex Hemphill's poetry in the second chapter of his award-winning *Evidence of Being: The Black Gay Cultural Renaissance and the Politics of Violence*. His analysis of Hemphill's writings emphasizes the poet's yearning for and envisioning of communal formations outside of the heteropatriarchal family. While my theorization of the Black Ecstatic eschews any commitment to the future as the site of promise or improvement or continuance even for those attempting to lead lives under the sign of blackness, it celebrates black communion and coming-together as methods for managing (if not ameliorating) the totalized social death that so negates black living. I find Bost's reading quite instructive in this regard.
54 Berlant, *Cruel Optimism*, 3.
55 Berlant, *Cruel Optimism*, 3.
56 See Holland, *Erotic Life of Racism*.

EPILOGUE. ON SUSTENANCE AND SUTURE

Epigraph: Butler, "Afterword," 468.

BIBLIOGRAPHY

Abdur-Rahman, Aliyyah I. *Against the Closet: Black Political Longing and the Erotics of Race*. Durham, NC: Duke University Press, 2012.

Abdur-Rahman, Aliyyah I. "'The Strangest Freaks of Despotism': Queer Sexuality in Antebellum African American Slave Narratives." *African American Review* 40, no. 2 (2006): 223–37.

Adorno, Theodor W. *Aesthetic Theory*. Minneapolis: University of Minnesota Press, 1997.

Ahmed, Sara. *The Cultural Politics of Emotion*. 2nd ed. Edinburgh: Edinburgh University Press, 2014.

Alexander, Michelle. *New Jim Crow: Mass Incarceration in the Age of Colorblindness*. New York: New Press, 2010.

Allen, Jafari S. *There's a Disco Ball between Us : A Theory of Black Gay Life*. Durham, NC: Duke University Press, 2021.

Allewaert, Monique. *Ariel's Ecology: Plantations, Personhood, and Colonialism in the American Tropics*. Minneapolis: University of Minnesota Press, 2013.

Alpers, Edward A. "The Idea of Marronage: Reflections on Literature and Politics in Réunion." *Slavery & Abolition* 25, no. 2 (August 2004): 18–29.

Anderson, Carol (Carol Elaine). *White Rage: The Unspoken Truth of Our Racial Divide*. New York: Bloomsbury, 2016.

Anderson, Devery S. *Emmett Till: The Murder That Shocked the World and Propelled the Civil Rights Movement*. Jackson: University Press of Mississippi, 2015.

Austin, J. L. *The Works of J. L. Austin*. Charlottesville, VA: InteLex, 2000.

Bakhtin, Mikhail. *Rabelais and His World*. Cambridge, MA: MIT Press, 1968.

Barber, Tiffany E., Angela Naimou, and Wangechi Mutu. "Between Disgust and Regeneration." *ASAP Journal* 1, no. 3 (2016): 337–63.

Barco, Mandalit del. "In *Moonlight*, Growing Up Black, Gay, and Poor in 1980s Miami." NPR, October 18, 2016. https://www.npr.org/2016/10/18/498358778/moonlight-coming-of-age-in-miami-during-the-war-on-drugs-era.

Barrett, Lindon. *Racial Blackness and the Discontinuity of Western Modernity*. Urbana: University of Illinois Press, 2014.

Berlant, Lauren. *Cruel Optimism*. Durham, NC: Duke University Press, 2011.

Berlant, Lauren. "The Subject of True Feeling: Pain, Privacy, and Politics." In *Cultural Studies and Political Theory*, edited by Jodi Dean, 42–62. Ithaca, NY: Cornell University Press, 2000.

Best, Stephen. *None Like Us: Blackness, Belonging, Aesthetic Life*. Durham, NC: Duke University Press, 2018.

Best, Stephen, and Saidiya Hartman. "Fugitive Justice." *Representations*, no. 92 (2005): 1–5.

Blackman, Marci. *Tradition*. Healdsburg, CA: Water Street, 2013.

Blackmon, Douglas A. *Slavery by Another Name: The Re-Enslavement of Black Americans from the Civil War to World War II*. New York: Anchor, 2009.

Bloch, Ernst. "Discussing Expressionism." Translated by Rodney Livingstone. In *Aesthetics and Politics*, by Ernst Bloch, Georg Lukács, Bertolt Brecht, Walter Benjamin, and Theodor Adorno, 16–27. London: NLB, 1977.

Bonilla-Silva, Eduardo. *Racism without Racists: Color-Blind Racism and the Persistence of Racial Inequality in America*. 5th ed. Lanham, MD: Rowman and Littlefield, 2018.

Borossa, Julia. "Identity, Loss, and the Mother Tongue." *Paragraph* 21, no. 3 (1998): 391–402.

Bost, Darius. *Evidence of Being: The Black Gay Cultural Renaissance and the Politics of Violence*. Chicago: University of Chicago Press, 2019.

brown, adrienne maree. *Pleasure Activism: The Politics of Feeling Good*. Chico, CA: AK, 2019.

Brown, Vincent. "Social Death and Political Life in the Study of Slavery." *American Historical Review* 114, no. 5 (2009): 1231–49.

Brown, Wendy. *Edgework: Critical Essays on Knowledge and Politics*. Princeton, NJ: Princeton University Press, 2005.

Brown, Wendy. *States of Injury: Power and Freedom in Late Modernity*. Princeton, NJ: Princeton University Press, 1995.

Brown, William Wells. "Lecture." Presented at the Female Anti-Slavery Society of Salem, Lyceum Hall, Salem, MA, November 14, 1847.

Bruce, La Marr Jurelle. *How to Go Mad without Losing Your Mind: Madness and Black Radical Creativity*. Durham, NC: Duke University Press, 2021.

Bürger, Peter. *Theory of the Avant-Garde*. Minneapolis: University of Minnesota Press, 1984.

Butler, Judith. "Afterword: After Loss, What Then?" In *Loss: The Politics of Mourning*, edited by David L. Eng and David Kazanjian, 464–74. Berkeley: University of California Press, 2003.

Butler, Judith. *Undoing Gender*. New York: Routledge, 2004.

Cacho, Lisa Marie. *Social Death: Racialized Rightlessness and the Criminalization of the Unprotected*. New York: New York University Press, 2012.

Carretta, Vincent. "Introduction." In *Thoughts and Sentiments on the Evil of Slavery and Other Writings*, by Ottobah Cugoano, ix–xxviii. New York: Penguin, 1999.

Caruth, Cathy. *Unclaimed Experience: Trauma, Narrative, and History.* Baltimore, MD: Johns Hopkins University Press, 1996.
Childs, Dennis. *Slaves of the State: Black Incarceration from the Chain Gang to the Penitentiary.* Minneapolis: University of Minnesota Press, 2015.
Claudia, Rankine. "The Condition of Black Life Is One of Mourning." In *The Fire This Time: A New Generation Speaks about Race,* edited by Jesmyn Ward, 145–56. New York: Scribner, 2016.
Cohen, Cathy J. *The Boundaries of Blackness: AIDS and the Breakdown of Black Politics.* Chicago: University of Chicago Press, 1999.
Corn, Marti, Tracy Xavia Karner, Thad Sitton, Tacey A. Rosolowski, and Wanda Horton-Woodworth. *The Ground on Which I Stand: Tamina, a Freedmen's Town.* Vol. 22. College Station: Texas A&M University Press, 2016.
Crawford, Margo Natalie. *Black Post-Blackness: the Black Arts Movement and Twenty-First-Century Aesthetics.* Urbana: University of Illinois Press, 2017.
Crawford, Margo Natalie. "The Inside-Turned-Out Architecture of the Post-Neo-Slave Narrative." In *The Psychic Hold of Slavery,* edited by Aida Levy-Hussen, Soyica Diggs Colbert, and Robert J. Patterson, 69–85. New Brunswick, NJ: Rutgers University Press, 2019.
Crawley, Ashon T. *Blackpentecostal Breath: The Aesthetics of Possibility.* New York: Fordham University Press, 2016.
Crimp, Douglas. "Mourning and Militancy." *October* 51 (1989): 3–18.
Cugoano, Ottobah. *Thoughts and Sentiments on the Evil of Slavery and Other Writings.* New York: Penguin, 1999.
da Silva, Denise Ferreira. "Hacking the Subject: Black Feminism and Refusal beyond the Limits of Critique." *philoSOPHIA* 8, no. 1 (2018): 19–41.
da Silva, Denise Ferreira. "To Be Announced: Radical Praxis or Knowing (at) the Limits of Justice." *Social Text* 31, no. 1 (March 1, 2013): 43–62.
da Silva, Denise Ferreira. "Toward a Black Feminist Poethics: The Quest(ion) of Blackness toward the End of the World." *Black Scholar* 44, no. 2 (2014): 81–97.
da Silva, Denise Ferreira. *Toward a Global Idea of Race.* Minneapolis: University of Minnesota Press, 2007.
Dayan, Colin. *The Law Is a White Dog: How Legal Rituals Make and Unmake Persons.* Princeton, NJ: Princeton University Press, 2011.
Dayan, Colin. "With Law at the Edge of Life." *South Atlantic Quarterly* 113, no. 3 (2014): 629–39.
Dean, Jodi. *Cultural Studies and Political Theory.* Ithaca, NY: Cornell University Press, 2000.
Deleuze, Gilles. *Difference and Repetition.* London: Continuum, 2001.
Derrida, Jacques. *Of Grammatology.* Translated by Gayatri Chakravorty Spivak. Rev. ed. Baltimore, MD: Johns Hopkins University Press, 1998.
Díaz, Junot. *The Brief Wondrous Life of Oscar Wao.* New York: Riverhead, 2007.
Douglass, Frederick. *Narrative of the Life of Frederick Douglass with Study Guide: Deluxe Special Edition.* New York: G&D Media, 2019.
Dove, Rita. *Grace Notes: Poems.* New York: W. W. Norton, 1991.

Duberman, Martin. *Hold Tight Gently: Michael Callen, Essex Hemphill, and the Battlefield of AIDS*. New York: New Press, 2014.

Du Bois, W. E. B. *The Souls of Black Folk by W. E. B. Du Bois: With a Critical Introduction by Patricia H. Hinchey*. Gorham, ME: Myers Education Press, 2018.

Duggan, Lisa. *The Twilight of Equality? Neoliberalism, Cultural Politics, and the Attack on Democracy*. Boston: Beacon, 2003.

Eng, David L., and David Kazanjian. *Loss: The Politics of Mourning*. Berkeley: University of California Press, 2003.

Fanon, Frantz. *Black Skin, White Masks*. New York: Grove, 1967.

Felman, Shoshana. "Theaters of Justice: Arendt in Jerusalem, the Eichmann Trial, and the Redefinition of Legal Meaning in the Wake of the Holocaust." *Theoretical Inquiries in Law* 1, no. 2 (2001): 8: 1–43.

Fink, Bruce. *The Lacanian Subject: Between Language and Jouissance*. Princeton, NJ: Princeton University Press, 1995.

Foster, Hal. *The Return of the Real: The Avant-Garde at the End of the Century*. Cambridge, MA: MIT Press, 1996.

Friedman, Gabriella. "Unsentimental Historicizing: The Neo-Slave Narrative Tradition and the Refusal of Feeling." *American Literature* 93, no. 1 (March 1, 2021): 115–43.

Fuentes, Marisa J. *Dispossessed Lives: Enslaved Women, Violence, and the Archive*. Philadelphia: University of Pennsylvania Press, 2016.

Ganteau, Jean-Michel, and Susana Onega Jaén. *Contemporary Trauma Narratives: Liminality and the Ethics of Form*. New York: Routledge, 2014.

Glissant, Édouard. *Caribbean Discourse: Selected Essays*. Edited by J. Michael Dash. Charlottesville: University of Virginia Press, 1999.

Glissant, Édouard. *Poetics of Relation*. Translated by Betsy Wing. Ann Arbor: University of Michigan Press, 1997.

Haley, Sarah. *No Mercy Here: Gender, Punishment, and the Making of Jim Crow Modernity*. Chapel Hill: University of North Carolina Press, 2016.

Harper, Phillip Brian. *Abstractionist Aesthetics: Artistic Form and Social Critique in African American Culture*. New York: New York University Press, 2015.

Hartman, Saidiya. "The Belly of the World: A Note on Black Women's Labors." *Souls* 18, no. 1 (2016): 166–73.

Hartman, Saidiya. *Lose Your Mother: A Journey along the Atlantic Slave Route*. New York: Farrar, Straus and Giroux, 2007.

Hartman, Saidiya. *Scenes of Subjection: Terror, Slavery, and Self-Making in Nineteenth-Century America*. New York: Oxford University Press, 1997.

Hartman, Saidiya. "Venus in Two Acts." *Small Axe* 12, no. 2 (June 2008): 1–14.

Hartman, Saidiya. *Wayward Lives, Beautiful Experiments: Intimate Histories of Social Upheaval*. New York: W. W. Norton, 2019.

Hemphill, Essex. *Ceremonies: Prose and Poetry*. New York: Plume, 1992.

Henderson, Mae G. *Speaking in Tongues and Dancing Diaspora: Black Women Writing and Performing*. Vol. 17. New York: Oxford University Press, 2014.

Hernandez, Jillian. "The Ambivalent Grotesque: Reading Black Women's Erotic Corporeality in Wangechi Mutu's Work." *Signs: Journal of Women in Culture and Society* 42, no. 2 (2017): 427–57.

Hirsch, Marianne. *The Generation of Postmemory: Writing and Visual Culture after the Holocaust.* New York: Columbia University Press, 2012.

Holiday, Harmony. "The Black Catatonic Scream." *Triple Canopy*, August 20, 2020. https://canopycanopycanopy.com/contents/the-black-catatonic-scream.

Holiday, Harmony, and Denise Lynée. "The Sound of Getting Out." Presented at the Omniaudience (Side Two), Coaxial Arts, Los Angeles, CA, May 5, 2019.

Holland, Sharon Patricia. *The Erotic Life of Racism.* Durham, NC: Duke University Press, 2012.

Holland, Sharon Patricia. *Raising the Dead Readings of Death and (Black) Subjectivity.* Durham, NC: Duke University Press, 2000.

hooks, bell. *Outlaw Culture: Resisting Representations.* New York: Routledge, 1994.

In the Middle. "Why History Matters Redux: The Redress Project." July 30, 2006. https://www.inthemedievalmiddle.com/2006/07/why-history-matters-redux-redress.html.

Jackson, Zakiyyah Iman. *Becoming Human Matter and Meaning in an Antiblack World.* New York: New York University Press, 2021.

Johnson, Sara E. *The Fear of French Negroes: Transcolonial Collaboration in the Revolutionary Americas.* Vol. 12. Berkeley: University of California Press, 2012.

Johnson, Walter. *Soul by Soul: Life inside the Antebellum Slave Market.* Cambridge, MA: Harvard University Press, 1999.

Jones, Martha S. *Birthright Citizens: A History of Race and Rights in Antebellum America.* Cambridge: Cambridge University Press, 2018.

Jones, Saeed. "Infinite Ache: My First Mother's Day without Her." *Ebony*, May 8, 2012 https://www.ebony.com/awe-my-first-mothers-day-without-her.

Jones, Saeed. *Prelude to Bruise: Poetry.* Minneapolis: Coffee House, 2014.

Jones, Shermaine M. "Presenting Our Bodies, Laying Our Case: The Political Efficacy of Grief and Rage during the Civil Rights Movement in Alice Walker's *Meridian*." *Southern Quarterly* 52, no. 1 (2014): 179–95.

Judy, Ronald A. T. *DisForming the American Canon: African-Arabic Slave Narratives and the Vernacular.* Minneapolis: University of Minnesota Press, 1993.

Kafka, Franz, and Max Brod. *The Blue Octavo Notebooks.* Cambridge, MA: Exact Change, 1991.

Keeling, Kara. *Queer Times, Black Futures.* New York: New York University Press, 2019.

Keene, John. *Annotations.* New York: New Directions, 1995.

Kendi, Ibram X. *Stamped from the Beginning: The Definitive History of Racist Ideas in America.* New York: Nation, 2016.

Kielian-Gilbert, Marianne. "Music and the Difference in Becoming." In *Sounding the Virtual: Gilles Deleuze and the Theory and Philosophy of Music*, 199–226. New York: Routledge, 2010.

La Berge, Leigh Claire. "The Rules of Abstraction." *Radical History Review*, no. 118 (Winter 2014): 93–112.

Lacan, Jacques. *The Seminar of Jacques Lacan: The Four Fundamental Concepts of Psychoanalysis.* Edited by Jacques-Alain Miller. Translated by Alan Sheridan. Rev. ed. New York: W. W. Norton, 1998.

LeFlouria, Talitha L. *Chained in Silence: Black Women and Convict Labor in the New South.* Chapel Hill: University of North Carolina Press, 2015.

Levy-Hussen, Aida. *How to Read African American Literature: Post–Civil Rights Fiction and the Task of Interpretation.* New York: New York University Press, 2016.

Levy-Hussen, Aida, Soyica Diggs Colbert, and Robert J. Patterson, eds. *The Psychic Hold of Slavery.* New Brunswick, NJ: Rutgers University Press, 2019.

Matthews, John T., and Aliyyah I. Abdur-Rahman. "What Moves at the Margin: William Faulkner and Race." In *The New Cambridge Companion to William Faulkner,* 44–58. Cambridge: Cambridge University Press, 2015.

Mbembe, Achille. *Necropolitics.* Translated by Steve Corcoran. Durham, NC: Duke University Press, 2019.

McDavid, Carol. "When Is 'Gone' Gone? Archaeology, Gentrification, and Competing Narratives about Freedmen's Town, Houston." *Historical Archaeology* 45, no. 3 (2011): 74–88.

McKittrick, Katherine. *Demonic Grounds: Black Women and the Cartographies of Struggle.* Minneapolis: University of Minnesota Press, 2006.

McKittrick, Katherine. "Mathematics, Black Life." *Black Scholar* 44, no. 2 (Summer 2014): 16–28.

McKittrick, Katherine. *Sylvia Wynter: On Being Human as Praxis.* Durham, NC: Duke University Press, 2015.

Melamed, Jodi. *Represent and Destroy Rationalizing Violence in the New Racial Capitalism.* Minneapolis: University of Minnesota Press, 2011.

Monet, Aja. *My Mother Was a Freedom Fighter.* Chicago: Haymarket, 2017.

Morrison, Toni. *Beloved.* New York: Vintage International, 2004. First published 1987 by Knopf (New York).

Morrison, Toni. *The Source of Self-Regard: Selected Essays, Speeches, and Meditations.* New York: Knopf, 2019.

Moten, Fred. *In the Break: The Aesthetics of the Black Radical Tradition.* Minneapolis: University of Minnesota Press, 2003.

Muñoz, José Esteban. *Cruising Utopia: The Then and There of Queer Futurity.* New York: New York University Press, 2009.

Nash, Jennifer C. *The Black Body in Ecstasy: Reading Race, Reading Pornography.* Durham, NC: Duke University Press, 2014.

Ochieng' Nyongó, Tavia Amolo. *Afro-Fabulations: The Queer Drama of Black Life.* New York: New York University Press, 2019.

Patterson, Orlando. *Slavery and Social Death: A Comparative Study.* Cambridge, MA: Harvard University Press, 1982.

Perry, Imani. *Vexy Thing: On Gender and Liberation.* Durham, NC: Duke University Press, 2018.

Pickens, Therí A. *Black Madness: Mad Blackness.* Durham, NC: Duke University Press, 2019.

Quashie, Kevin Everod. *The Sovereignty of Quiet: Beyond Resistance in Black Culture.* New Brunswick, NJ: Rutgers University Press, 2012.

Reed, Anthony. *Freedom Time: The Poetics and Politics of Black Experimental Writing.* Baltimore, MD: Johns Hopkins University Press, 2014.

Reid-Pharr, Robert F. "At Home in America." In *Black Gay Man*, 62–82. New York: New York University Press, 2022.

Reynolds, Pamela. "Alexandria Smith's First Solo Boston Show Navigates the Duality of Existence." WBUR, November 5, 2018. https://www.wbur.org/news/2018/11/05/alexandria-smith-litany-for-survival-boston.

Roberts, Dorothy E. *Fatal Invention: How Science, Politics, and Big Business Re-Create Race in the Twenty-First Century.* New York: New Press, 2011.

Roberts, Neil. *Freedom as Marronage.* Chicago: University of Chicago Press, 2015.

Rodriguez, Dylan. *Forced Passages: Imprisoned Radical Intellectuals and the U.S. Prison Regime.* Minneapolis: University of Minnesota Press, 2006.

Samuels, Shirley. *The Culture of Sentiment: Race, Gender, and Sentimentality in Nineteenth-Century America.* New York: Oxford University Press, 1993.

Scott, Darieck. *Extravagant Abjection Blackness, Power, and Sexuality in the African American Literary Imagination.* New York: New York University Press, 2010.

Seshadri, Kalpana. *HumAnimal Race, Law, Language.* Minneapolis: University of Minnesota Press, 2012.

Sexton, Jared Yates. *Black Masculinity and the Cinema of Policing.* Cham: Palgrave Macmillan, 2017.

Sexton, Jared Yates. "People-of-Color-Blindness." *Social Text* 28, no. 2 (2010): 31–56.

Sexton, Jared Yates. "The Social Life of Social Death: On Afro-Pessimism and Black Optimism." *InTensions*, no. 5 (Fall–Winter 2011): 1–47.

Sharpe, Christina Elizabeth. *In the Wake: On Blackness and Being.* Durham, NC: Duke University Press, 2016.

Sharpe, Christina Elizabeth. *Monstrous Intimacies: Making Post-Slavery Subjects.* Durham, NC: Duke University Press, 2010.

Smallwood, Stephanie E. *Saltwater Slavery: A Middle Passage from Africa to American Diaspora.* Cambridge, MA: Harvard University Press, 2007.

Spillers, Hortense. "Mama's Baby, Papa's Maybe: An American Grammar Book." *Diacritics* 17, no. 2 (Summer 1987): 65–81.

Spillers, Hortense. "Women and the Early Republics: Revolution, Sentiment, and Sorrow." Presented at the W. E. B. Du Bois Lecture, Harvard University, Hutchins Center, Cambridge, MA, October 14, 2014.

Stoler, Ann Laura. *Duress: Imperial Durabilities in Our Times.* Durham, NC: Duke University Press, 2016.

Sullivan, Mecca Jamilah. *The Poetics of Difference: Queer Feminist Forms in the African Diaspora.* Urbana: University of Illinois Press, 2021.

Taylor, Keeanga-Yamahtta. *From #BlackLivesMatter to Black Liberation.* Chicago: Haymarket, 2016.

Tariq, Malcolm. *Heed the Hollow: Poems.* Minneapolis: Graywolf, 2019.

Veaux, Alexis De. *Yabo.* Washington, DC: RedBone, 2014.

Voegelin, Salomé. *Listening to Noise and Silence towards a Philosophy of Sound Art.* New York: Continuum, 2010.

Walker, Alice. *The Way Forward Is with a Broken Heart.* New York: Random House, 2000.

Wang, Jackie. *Carceral Capitalism.* South Pasadena, CA: Semiotexte, 2018.

Ward, Jesmyn. *The Fire This Time: A New Generation Speaks about Race.* New York: Scribner, 2016.

Weheliye, Alexander G. *Habeas Viscus: Racializing Assemblages, Biopolitics, and Black Feminist Theories of the Human.* Durham, NC: Duke University Press, 2014.

Weinstein, Cindy. "The Slave Narrative and Sentimental Literature." In *The Cambridge Companion to the African American Slave Narrative*, 115–34. New York: Cambridge University Press, 2007.

Whitehead, Colson. *The Underground Railroad.* New York: Doubleday, 2016.

Wilder, Gary. "Making Freedom Time." *History of the Present* 7, no. 1 (Spring 2017): 122–37.

Wilderson, Frank B. *Red, White, and Black: Cinema and the Structure of U.S. Antagonisms.* Durham, NC: Duke University Press, 2010.

Woubshet, Dagmawi. *The Calendar of Loss: Race, Sexuality, and Mourning in the Early Era of AIDS.* Baltimore, MD: Johns Hopkins University Press, 2015.

Wright, Michelle M. *Physics of Blackness: Beyond the Middle Passage Epistemology.* Minneapolis: University of Minnesota Press, 2015.

Wynter, Sylvia. "Unsettling the Coloniality of Being/Power/Truth/Freedom: Towards the Human, After Man, Its Overrepresentation—An Argument." *CR: The New Centennial Review* 3, no. 3 (2003): 257–337.

Yates-Richard, Meina. "'What Is Your Mother's Name?': Maternal Disavowal and the Reverberating Aesthetic of Black Women's Pain in Black Nationalist Literature." *American Literature* 88, no. 3 (2016): 477–507.

Young, Harvey. *Embodying Black Experience: Stillness, Critical Memory, and the Black Body.* Ann Arbor: University of Michigan Press, 2010.

INDEX

Page numbers in *italics* refer to figures.

www.ingramcontent.com/pod-product-compliance
Lightning Source LLC
LaVergne TN
LVHW050957080826
845145LV00009B/2335